A Research Guide for Undergraduate Students
English and American Literature

Third Edition

Nancy L. Baker

The Modern Language Association of America
New York 1989

Acknowledgments

Abstracts of English Studies for *Abstracts of English Studies*. ☐ English Association for *The Year's Work in English Studies*. ☐ Gale Research Inc. for *Book Review Index*, vol. 23, no. 6, edited by Barbara Beach, Gale Research Inc., 1988. Copyright © 1988 by Gale Research Company; reprinted by permission of the publisher. ☐ G. K. Hall & Co. for Joseph M. Kuntz and Nancy C. Martinez, *Poetry Explication*. Copyright © 1980 and reprinted with the permission of G. K. Hall & Co., Boston. ☐ Harvard University Press for Marvin Spevack, *The Harvard Concordance to Shakespeare*. Reprinted by permission. ☐ Modern Humanities Research Association for *Annual Bibliography of English Language and Literature*. ☐ Oxford University Press for *Oxford English Dictionary*, 1933. ☐ Princeton University Press for Alex Preminger et al., eds., *Princeton Encyclopedia of Poetry and Poetics*. Copyright © 1965, enlarged edition copyright © 1974, by Princeton University Press. Reprinted with permission of Princeton University Press. ☐ Scarecrow Press, Inc., for *Literary Criticism Index*. ☐ Shoe String Press for Helen H. Palmer and Anne J. Dyson, *English Novel Explication*, and Warren S. Walker, *Twentieth-Century Short Story Explication*. ☐ Phillip Thomson for *An Index to Book Reviews in the Humanities*. ☐ H. W. Wilson Company for *Bibliographic Index*, copyright © 1986 by the H. W. Wilson Company; *Book Review Digest*, copyright © 1987 by the H. W. Wilson Company; *Essay and General Literature Index*, copyright © 1985 by the H. W. Wilson Company; *Humanities Index*, copyright © 1987 by the H. W. Wilson Company. Material reproduced by permission of the publisher.

Library of Congress Cataloging-in-Publication Data

Baker. Nancy L., 1950–
    A research guide for undergraduate students : English and American
    literature / Nancy L. Baker. — 3rd ed.
        p.   cm.
    Bibliography: p.
    ISBN 0-87352-186-2
    1. English Literature — Research — Methodology.   2. Bibliography —
Bibliography — English literature.   3. English literature —
Bibliography.   4. American literature — Research — Methodology.
5. Bibliography — Bibliography — American literature.   6. American
literature — Bibliography.   I. Title.
PR56.B34   1989
807.2 — dc19   89-31005

Published by The Modern Language Association of America
10 Astor Place, New York, New York 10003–6981

Contents

Preface to the Third Edition   2

Preface to the Second Edition   2

Introduction   4

1. Bibliographies: A Good Beginning   6
2. Combing the Catalog   10
3. Finding Parts of Books   18
4. Locating Articles in Periodicals   20
5. Using Annual Bibliographies   24
6. Special Indexes and Bibliographies
    a. Bibliographies by Genre   36
    b. Bibliographies by Literary Period   39
    c. Indexes to Book Reviews   39
7. Other Reference Tools
    a. Biographical Sources   43
    b. In Quest of Quotations   44
    c. Facts from Dictionaries and Handbooks   45
    d. Guidelines on Form   47
8. Using Other Libraries   49
9. Guides to Research in Literature   50

Appendix:
Selective Bibliography of Reference
Sources for English and American Literature   51

Preface to the Third Edition

My remarks in the preface to the second edition of this guide remain so true that I have asked the publisher to reprint them here. The computer revolution in our society and in libraries continues to spawn new products, such as the CD–ROM (compact disk — read only memory), and new services for patrons. But the latest innovations brought about by the computer are mainly frosting on a cake that I described in the earlier preface.

This is not to say that the changes made in the third edition are negligible. Once again I have revised chapter 5 stem to stern, and I have added many illustrations throughout the text. Chapters 2 and 4 read very differently, too.

For this edition of *A Research Guide for Undergraduate Students: English and American Literature*, I would like to acknowledge my colleagues Timothy Jewell, Online Reference Librarian, and all the reference librarians at the University of Washington Libraries. I also must recognize Charles A. Carpenter, professor of English at the State University of New York, Binghamton; the readers and editors at the Modern Language Association; and, of course, my husband and online editor, James Baker.

As a third edition would imply, I have been gratified by the success of my modest guide for undergraduate students. I hope that this little book continues to prove profitable to its readers.

N. L. B.
University of Washington

Preface to the Second Edition

When I began writing this literary research guide for undergraduate students, I suspected that a revised edition would become inevitable sometime in the misty future. But I never imagined how soon "Second Edition" would have to be printed on the title page.

Besides the passage of time, which, like the wind and the rain, erodes all things eventually, the main culprit is the computer. Just as the machine that *Time* magazine elected "man of the year" revolutionizes our society almost by the hour, small and relatively inexpensive computers are transforming, even mechanizing, such a humanistic pursuit as literary research.

It would be difficult to conceive of a more powerful and efficient tool for producing bibliographies than the microcomputer. The machine's proliferation has meant more and better reference books for all researchers, including undergraduate students. I am thinking of new books like *Literary Criticism Index* and of the many supplements to bibliographies discussed in chapter 6 of this guide.

The best example would have to be the *MLA Bibliography*. At the same time that the Modern Language Association (MLA) was publishing my research guide in 1982, it was releasing the latest volume of its indispensable bibliography, which had a totally new format. Electronic automation made possible the many significant improvements in the *MLA Bibliography* for 1981 and later years, necessitating a top-to-bottom revision of chapter 5 in my research guide. Readers of this guide's first edition must have felt somewhat baffled by the MLA volumes after 1980. It is my hope that confusion not be the lot of readers of the second edition.

Computers are nothing new in libraries. For more than a decade, technical operations like book acquisitions and cataloging have been increasingly automated in order to save time and bolster accuracy. Now that computers cost less (and people use the machines more), electronic automation is moving out into the public part — that is, your part — of the library. The card catalog at your college or university library may have gone online already or will do so very soon. Instead of leafing through cards in drawers, you will manipulate the keys on a computer console. Meanwhile, data-base services like Dialog and Wilsonline have opened the door to research by computer.

The temptation for me in revising this research guide was simply to add a chapter on electronic automation, which would have outlined the computer revolution in libraries. I decided such an addition would be too easy and, in a way, dishonest. If your library has an online system, the computer is the card catalog. You need to know that, and I need to deal with that right in chapter 2, not at some later point. Although the tables of contents are the same, there are numerous changes — some subtle, others not so subtle — between the texts of the two editions of this guide.

As I did in the first edition, I would like to acknowledge Charles A. Carpenter, professor of English, State University of New York, Binghamton, who helped and encouraged me with the original concept for this book. For the second edition, I want to recognize the inestimable assistance of the Reference Department, Suzzallo Library, University of Washington. And, as always, I owe a great debt of gratitude to my husband, James Baker, who continues to edit my words without mercy and to support my projects without fail. I would also like to thank the readers and editors at the Modern Language Association.

Yes, I did write, edit, and print out this second edition to *A Research Guide for Undergraduate Students* on my personal computer. The typewriter that tapped out the manuscript for the first edition now gathers dust in the corner.

N. L. B.
University of Washington

Introduction

This brief guide to research methods in English and American literature is written for you, the undergraduate student. Most other research guides to literature are written for graduate students and advanced scholars, who have more experience with the library and who may need exhaustive lists of numerous specialized reference works. None of the other guides effectively deals with your problems as a library user.

My experience as a reference librarian has convinced me that your research requirements are special. Because your time and the scope of your work are both limited, you are unlikely to need many of the specialized reference sources in your library. But most undergraduate students are not familiar enough with the basic tools and the organization of the library to use their time there efficiently. They often leave frustrated and angry. If they cannot find material on a subject, they conclude that the library doesn't have it. Almost always they're wrong; they simply don't know how to locate what they want.

Keeping this in mind, you should not be surprised that this guide is restricted to the search for secondary sources, those materials that analyze and criticize an author's work. As an undergraduate you rarely, if ever, deal with problems involving primary sources — for example, the various editions of an author's works. This guide stresses the thirty or so literary research tools that are most likely to be useful to you. An annotated list of about sixty-five others is appended for further study.

This guide also discusses basic research strategy. It presents a systematic way of locating important books and articles on English and American literature. Such a search involves more than just thumbing through the card catalog, if your library still has such a catalog. To be thorough, you should seek all pertinent bibliographies and indexes of articles, as well as all important books, on a subject. Then, even though many of these articles and books prove irrelevant to your topic, you can be confident that you have not overlooked any major studies. Moreover, by structuring your research systematically, you can spend most of your time in writing the term paper rather than in searching for materials.

This guide is arranged to outline an orderly approach to researching a term-paper topic, from the assembling of a preliminary bibliography to the proper typing of documentation in the finished paper. Chapters 1 and 2 offer advice on compiling a list of materials, chapters 2 through 6 concern looking for the materials, and chapters 7 through 9 touch on reference tools and library resources that save time and solve problems arising during your search. The appendix lists about sixty-five reference tools you might wish to consult for more complicated and specialized topics. To demonstrate the use of the various reference sources, I have selected *Hamlet*, by William Shakespeare; "To Autumn," by John Keats; and *Tar Baby*, by Toni Morrison. These works permit me to illustrate research in three genres and three historical periods. For a study of a literary theme or movement, as opposed to a specific author or work, I have chosen the sample topic "the stereotypical characterization of blacks in American fiction." At times, I have also found it appropriate to use other works, authors, and topics as examples of particular points.

The research process is a fluid one. No single strategy is entirely successful for every problem. In suggesting a systematic approach to research on a conventional term-paper topic, I do not mean to reduce a creative and interpretative process to a rigid lockstep. For some research problems, certain chapters of this guide do not apply at all. For many topics, the sources discussed in the first five chapters may provide all the literary criticism you can handle. Individual problems require their own research strategies. From this guide you should gain a basic understanding of what various types of reference sources can and cannot do; a working familiarity with the major indexes, bibliographies, and other research tools in literature; and an idea of systematic research methods. The quality of your term papers should improve along with the efficiency and productivity of your research efforts.

I.
Bibliographies
A Good Beginning

The most efficient way to begin your research is to determine whether a good bibliography of literary criticism is available on your subject. Such a publication, which may have appeared as a book, a part of a book, or an article in a periodical, can expedite your search and reduce the possibility of your overlooking major critical studies pertinent to your topic. In addition, it can act as a timesaving checklist for later steps in the research process, such as investigating your library's holdings on your subject. If few of the works listed are available, you may wish to change your topic — before it's too late — to one on which your library has more material. If you don't want to change your subject, you may have to use other libraries as well, and you need to plan your time accordingly (see ch. 8).

Although extremely useful, a published bibliography should not be your only research tool. Most bibliographies are selective, making no attempt to list all the works on a particular subject. Even the most ambitious cannot cover material that appears after they have gone to press; you are going to have to update the listings.

Bibliographies are most easily found in three basic sources: bibliographies of bibliographies, the card or online catalog, and standard literary indexes and bibliographies. For the remainder of this chapter, we will look at bibliographies of bibliographies.

One extremely convenient bibliography of bibliographies is the *Literary Criticism Index*, by Weiner and Means. In recent years, there has been a noticeable growth in reference books that list literary criticism (see ch. 6), so that the value of a single index to all the various bibliographies has become increasingly apparent. Recognition of this need led to the publication of the *Literary Criticism Index*.

Let's assume, to demonstrate its usefulness, that you want to track down discussions of Keats's "To Autumn." The *Literary Criticism Index* will refer you to specific pages in four bibliographies, each represented by an abbreviation (fig. 1). Using the key to abbreviations in the front of the book (fig. 2), you will discover, for example, that one list of criticism of Keats's poem appears on pages 274–75 of *Poetry Explication*. Although some smaller college libraries may not own all the bibliographies covered by the *Literary Criticism Index*, most institutions undoubtedly carry enough of them to warrant at least a quick initial consultation of this reference work.

KEATS, John

General EDT: 202-203; Fog: 38-41; ICBAP: 74; LCAB: 104; Ma: 1117-1119; Re: 174-183

"La Belle Dame Sans Merci" Fog: 42-43; ICBAP: 74; LCAB: 104; PE: 262; Re: 177-178

"Bright Star" PE: 262

"Endymion" Fog: 43; ICBAP: 74; LCAB: 104; Re: 178, 180, 183

"Epistle to Charles Cowden Clarke" PE: 263

Epistle to John Hamilton Reynolds Fog: 43

"The Eve of St. Agnes" Fog: 43-44; ICBAP: 74; LCAB: 104; PE: 263-264; Re: 177-178, 180, 183

"The Eve of St. Mark" PE: 264

"Fairy's Song" PE: 264

"The Fall of Hyperion" Fog: 44; ICBAP: 74; PE: 264-265; Re: 178-179

"The Great Odes" Fog: 41; Re: 179, 182-183

"Hyperion" Fog: 44-45; PE: 265; Re: 178-179, 182

"I Stood Tip-toe" Fog: 45; PE: 266

• • •

"Ode to Psyche" Fog: 42; ICBAP: 75; PE: 273

"On First Looking into Chapman's Homer" ICBAP: 75; PE: 273-274

"On Seeing the Elgin Marbles for the First Time" PE: 274

"On Sitting Down to Read King Lear Once Again" ICBAP: 75; PE: 274

"On Visiting the Tomb of Burns" PE: 274

"Sleep and Poetry" Fog: 45; ICBAP: 75; PE: 274

"To Autumn" Fog: 41; ICBAP: 75; PE: 274-275; Re: 181-182

Fig. 1. *Literary Criticism Index* 330–31.

xvi / Key to Symbols

NI — Logan, Terence P. The New Intellectuals: A Survey and Bibliography of Recent Studies in English Renaissance Drama. Lincoln, Nebraska: University of Nebraska Press, 1977.

OMEP — Beale, Walter H. Old and Middle English Poetry: A Guide to Information Sources. Detroit: Gale Research Company, 1976.

PE — Kuntz, Joseph M. Poetry Explication: A Checklist of Interpretation Since 1925 of British and American Poems Past and Present. Boston: G. K. Hall, 1980.

Po — Pownall, David E. Articles on Twentieth Century Literature: An Annotated Bibliography, 1954 to 1970. New York: Kraus-Thomson Organization Limited, 1973.

Fig. 2. *Literary Criticism Index* xvi.

One of the best cumulative bibliographies of bibliographies is the *Biblio-graphic Index*. Published three times a year and combined annually into one volume, it lists substantial bibliographies, of fifty citations or more, on a large variety of subjects. It covers bibliographies published as books, in books, and in over two thousand periodicals.

If, for example, you were to consult the 1986 *Bibliographic Index*, in research-ing a paper on the stereotypical characterization of blacks in American fic-tion, you would find a promising citation under the heading "Afro-Americans in literature" (fig. 3): the bibliography on pages 241–47 of *Amalgamation! Race, Sex, and Rhetoric in the Nineteenth-Century American Novel*, by James Kinney.

Again, if you consulted the 1986 *Bibliographic Index* for a bibliography of criticism about "To Autumn," by John Keats, you would find a bibliogra-phy cited under the author's name (fig. 4). The first entry under the sub-heading "By and about" shows that the *Keats-Shelley Journal* published substantial current bibliographies during each of the preceding three years.

After checking several years of the *Bibliographic Index* under "Shakespeare, William," you will undoubtedly notice that the last issue of each year of the *Shakespeare Quarterly* has an annotated bibliography. Many periodicals offer annual bibliographies of scholarship on appropriate authors, literary periods, or genres. An annual bibliography for contemporary drama ap-pears in *Modern Drama*; one for the Romantic period was a supplement to *English Language Notes* between 1964 and 1978. Many, but not all, of the peri-odicals that feature these bibliographies are indexed in the *Bibliographic In-dex*. Those not among the thousand periodicals covered there can be found through the standard literary indexes and bibliographies discussed in chap-ters 4 and 5.

The publisher of the *Bibliographic Index*, H. W. Wilson, has developed com-puterized versions for most of its indexes through an online retrieval system called Wilsonline and a CD–ROM (compact disk — read only memory) ver-sion called Wilsondisc. These automated editions of the *Bibliographic Index*, however, include only the volumes since November 1984. For more about retrieving bibliographic citations by computer, please turn to chapters 2 and 4.

Afro-Americans in literature
   See also
      American literature—Afro-American authors
   Kinney, James. Amalgamation!; race, sex, and rhetoric
      in the nineteenth-century American novel. (Contribu-
      tions in Afro-American and African studies, no90)
      Greenwood Press 1985 p241-7
   Watson, Carole McAlpine. Prologue; the novels of Black
      American women, 1891-1965. (Contributions in
      American studies, no79) Greenwood Press 1985 p129-59
   Yancy; Preston M. The Afro-American short story; a
      comprehensive, annotated index with selected commen-
      taries. (Bibliographies and indexes in Afro-American
      and African studies, no10) Greenwood Press 1986 171p

Fig. 3. *Bibliographic Index* 26: 12.

Keats, John, 1795-1821—About—*cont.*
   Shelley, Percy Bysshe. Shelley's Adonais; a critical edition
      [by] Anthony D. Knerr. Columbia Univ. Press 1984
      p271-82
                  By and about
   Current bibliography. *Keats-Shelley J* 33:244-68 '84;
      34:212-31 '85; 35:233-68 '86
   Goslee, Nancy Moore. Uriel's eye; Miltonic stationing
      and statuary in Blake, Keats, and Shelley. University
      of Ala. Press 1985 p233-55

Fig. 4. *Bibliographic Index* 26: 361.

2.
Combing the Catalog

Whether or not you have a bibliography from the *Bibliographic Index* or the *Literary Criticism Index* in hand, you will need to become familiar with your library's listing of the books and periodicals in its collection. A card catalog has traditionally served this purpose, but your library may have replaced its card catalog with a bank of computer terminals, microcomputers, or some other machinery that allows you to access an electronic listing of its holdings. If a library is in the process of creating an online catalog, it must keep the card catalog available alongside the new online catalog until all the old titles have been entered into the data base. In this case, you must check both catalogs to make sure that you have not overlooked pertinent materials. Some libraries, not yet bitten by the automation bug, still have traditional card catalogs. Since online catalogs have evolved from their printed predecessors, the two have many features in common. An understanding of the way traditional card catalogs are organized can help you use their electronic counterparts effectively. For this reason, a discussion of how to use the card catalog should be beneficial even if your library has an online catalog. To avoid confusion, I use the term *card catalog* to refer to the traditional printed version where cards are filed in cabinets, the term *online catalog* for those stored and accessed electronically, and the single term *catalog* for either one.

When you find potentially useful books cited in the bibliographies discussed in chapter 1, you can check the catalog under their authors or titles to determine whether your library has them and, if it does, to secure their call numbers. An author or title search in the catalog is likely to be fairly straightforward.

A thorough subject search, however, can be more roundabout. Despite what many students assume, there is rarely only one appropriate subject heading that will lead to all pertinent books on a topic. On any given subject in English or American literature, a relevant work is likely to be listed under the name of the author, the literary period in which it was written, and a variety of other headings. If you are creative with subject headings, you can undoubtedly discover many books you might otherwise miss.

Most of the time, you are going to be looking for literary criticism on a specific work, and so you begin by checking the catalog under the author's name. If you look for literary criticism on *Hamlet* under the general heading "Shakespeare, William, 1564–1616," you may be confronted either with several drawers of cards or with screen after screen on your computer terminal listing books of literary criticism. Instead of sorting through all these entries, you may want to turn to the *Library of Congress Subject Headings*, a two-volume guide to the subject headings used by the Library of Congress, which is a model for most large libraries. Usually shelved near the catalog, this guide does not list personal names, since these are the obvious headings to check for material on particular authors or their works. Shakespeare, the one exception to this rule, is included to demonstrate the kinds of subdivisions that can be used with an author's name (fig. 5). Under the heading "Shakespeare, William, 1564–1616 — Bibliography," you might find a critical bibliography that could be a useful starting point for your research. Books about Shakespeare's treatment of women are listed under the heading "Shakespeare, William, 1564–1616 — Characters — Women." An important subdivision is " — Criticism and interpretation," which is often used after the name to identify studies concerned with more than one of the author's works. You should familiarize yourself with these subdivisions. They may be appropriate for any author in English and American literature.

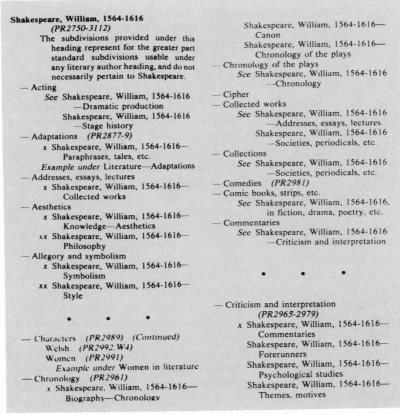

Shakespeare, William, 1564-1616
    (PR2750-3112)
    The subdivisions provided under this heading represent for the greater part standard subdivisions usable under any literary author heading, and do not necessarily pertain to Shakespeare.
— Acting
    See Shakespeare, William, 1564-1616
        —Dramatic production
    Shakespeare, William, 1564-1616
        —Stage history
— Adaptations *(PR2877-9)*
    x Shakespeare, William, 1564-1616—
        Paraphrases, tales, etc.
    Example under Literature—Adaptations
— Addresses, essays, lectures
    x Shakespeare, William, 1564-1616—
        Collected works
— Aesthetics
    x Shakespeare, William, 1564-1616—
        Knowledge—Aesthetics
    xx Shakespeare, William, 1564-1616—
        Philosophy
— Allegory and symbolism
    x Shakespeare, William, 1564-1616—
        Symbolism
    xx Shakespeare, William, 1564-1616—
        Style

        •   •   •

— Characters *(PR2989)* *(Continued)*
    Welsh *(PR2992.W4)*
    Women *(PR2991)*
        Example under Women in literature
— Chronology *(PR2961)*
    x Shakespeare, William, 1564-1616—
        Biography—Chronology

Shakespeare, William, 1564-1616—
    Canon
Shakespeare, William, 1564-1616—
    Chronology of the plays
— Chronology of the plays
    See Shakespeare, William, 1564-1616
        —Chronology
— Cipher
— Collected works
    See Shakespeare, William, 1564-1616
        —Addresses, essays, lectures
    Shakespeare, William, 1564-1616
        —Societies, periodicals, etc.
— Collections
    See Shakespeare, William, 1564-1616
        —Societies, periodicals, etc.
— Comedies *(PR2981)*
— Comic books, strips, etc.
    See Shakespeare, William, 1564-1616,
        in fiction, drama, poetry, etc.
— Commentaries
    See Shakespeare, William, 1564-1616
        —Criticism and interpretation

        •   •   •

— Criticism and interpretation
    (PR2965-2979)
    x Shakespeare, William, 1564-1616—
        Commentaries
    Shakespeare, William, 1564-1616—
        Forerunners
    Shakespeare, William, 1564-1616—
        Psychological studies
    Shakespeare, William, 1564-1616—
        Themes, motives

Fig. 5. *Library of Congress Subject Headings*, 10th ed. 2: 2894, 2896.

Literary criticism on a specific book appears in the catalog under the name of the author and the title of the work (fig. 6). Thus a 258–page study of madness in *Hamlet* can be found under the subject heading "Shakespeare, William, 1564–1616. Hamlet." The card itself provides additional clues for using the card catalog effectively. Besides giving you the call number and basic bibliographic information (i.e., author, title, place of publication, publisher, and date of publication), it informs you that Lidz's book includes a bibliography on pages 243–46. (From the bibliography you might derive the titles of other pertinent studies.) On the bottom of the card are all the subject headings and other entries under which Lidz's book appears in the card catalog. (Some libraries print these tracings, as they are called, on the backs of the cards.) The same information is generally shown for each entry in an online catalog, although the screen may not look exactly like a card. Lidz's book has the following tracings:

> Shakespeare, William, 1564–1616. Hamlet.
> Mental illness in literature.
> Shakespeare, William, 1564–1616. Hamlet — Sources.
> Psychoanalysis and literature.
> Title.

Altogether this book shows up in six places in the card catalog: under "Lidz, Theodore," under the book's title, and under four subject headings.

Let's consider another example. Cox's 1973 study of the dumb show in *Hamlet* can be found in the card catalog in four places: under Cox's name as author, under the book's title, and under two subject headings: "Shakespeare, William, 1564–1616. Hamlet" and "Pantomime" (fig. 7). If you decide to focus your paper on the dumb show in *Hamlet*, you might want to check the catalog for general books on the use and meaning of pantomime. The *Library of Congress Subject Headings* lists "Pantomime" as a legitimate heading (fig. 8), but the subject might not have occurred to you before you found Cox's book. As you can see, the Library of Congress guide often suggests other related headings. The "sa" (see also) references for "Pantomime" are "Ballet," "Happening (Art)," "Harlequin," "Mime," "Pantaloon (Fictitious character)," "Pantomime (Christmas entertainment)," and "Pierrot."

The guide also regularly supplies the general call numbers assigned to books on a given subject. Thus it informs you that books dealing with the history and criticism of pantomime in drama are shelved at PN 1985, an area of the collection in which you might want to browse. Book collections in libraries are organized by common subjects; books on the same subject theoretically have the same general call numbers. This is true for the Dewey Decimal system of book classification (with which you may already be familiar) as well as for the Library of Congress system. Although browsing

Shakespeare, William, 1564–1616. Hamlet.

Lidz, Theodore.
Hamlet's enemy : madness and myth in Hamlet / Theodore
Lidz. — New York : Basic Books, [1975]
PR 2807 L5 1975
xiii, 258 p. : ill. ; 24 cm.
Bibliography: p. 243-246.
Includes index.
ISBN 0-465-02817-9
1. Shakespeare, William, 1564-1616. Hamlet. 2. Mental illness in litera-
ture. 3. Shakespeare, William, 1564-1616. Hamlet—Sources. 4. Psychoa-
nalysis and literature. I. Title.
[DNLM: 1. Psychoanalytic interpretation. 2. Medicine in literature
WM49 L715h]
PR2807.L5   1975   822.3'3   74-25906
                                    75   MARC

Fig. 6. Library of Congress catalog card.

Shakespeare, William, 1564–1616. Hamlet.

Cox, Lee Sheridan.
Figurative design in Hamlet: the significance of the
dumb show. [Columbus] Ohio State University Press [1973]
PR 2807 C68
x, 184 p. 21 cm.
Includes bibliographical references.
1. Shakespeare, William, 1564-1616. Hamlet. 2. Pantomime.
I. Title.
PR2807.C68   822.3'3   72-12916
ISBN 0-8142-0175-X   MARC

Fig. 7. Library of Congress catalog card.

Pantomime *(Indirect) (Drama,*
PN1985-1988; Music, ML3460)
Here are entered works dealing with the
history or criticism of pantomime. Col-
lections of pantomimes are entered un-
der the heading Pantomimes.
sa Ballet
Happening (Art)
Harlequin
Mime
Pantaloon (Fictitious character)
Pantomime (Christmas entertainment)
Pierrot
x Dumb shows
xx Acting
Ballet
Drama
Gesture
Mime
Sign language
Theater
Note under Pantomimes

Fig. 8. *Library of Congress Subject Headings* 2: 2342–43.

can sometimes be productive, a random exploration of the bookshelves is no substitute for a systematic search of the catalog and appropriate reference sources. Some books related to your subject may be off the shelves at the time you browse, or they may be classified elsewhere. No classification system is perfect, and books with common subjects do not always fall as closely together as you might expect.

Before you finish searching the catalog for books on *Hamlet*, you may want to check for books dealing with English Renaissance drama or even English Renaissance literature. If you look under the headings "English drama" and "English literature" in the Library of Congress guide (figs. 9 and 10), you will see that they are subdivided by time and by a variety of other qualifications. Books about Elizabethan drama and literature are probably going to be too general for your purposes. A good bibliography in either Elizabethan drama or Elizabethan literature, however, might well prove helpful. Such bibliographies are found under two subject headings:

> English drama — Early modern and Elizabethan,
> 1500–1600 — Bibliography.
> English literature — Early modern, 1500–1700 — Bibliography.

The subdivision " — Bibliography" can be assigned to any subject heading. A bibliography on pantomime would be listed under "Pantomime — Bibliography." You should also become familiar with the various subdivisions used with the headings "English literature" and "American literature."

In sum, for your term paper on *Hamlet*, you should consult the card catalog under the following headings:

> Shakespeare, William, 1564–1616. Hamlet.
> Shakespeare, William, 1564–1616 — Bibliography.
> Shakespeare, William, 1564–1616 — Criticism and interpretation.

Other possibilities include the headings for the English drama and the English literature of Shakespeare's time and any specific subjects, such as "Pantomime," that may be suggested by tracings or that come to mind as your topic becomes more concrete.

You would use similar headings for other subjects in English and American literature. For a paper on the stereotypical characterization of blacks in American fiction, you would consult the catalog under the headings:

> Afro-Americans in literature.
> American fiction — 19th century — History and criticism.
> American fiction — 20th century — History and criticism.

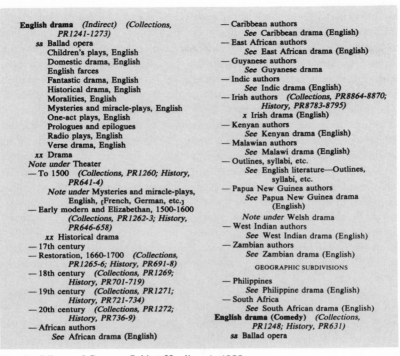

English drama *(Indirect)* *(Collections, PR1241-1273)*
- *sa* Ballad opera
  Children's plays, English
  Domestic drama, English
  English farces
  Fantastic drama, English
  Historical drama, English
  Moralities, English
  Mysteries and miracle-plays, English
  One-act plays, English
  Prologues and epilogues
  Radio plays, English
  Verse drama, English
- *xx* Drama
  Note under Theater
- — To 1500 *(Collections, PR1260; History, PR641-4)*
  Note under Mysteries and miracle-plays, English, [French, German, etc.]
- — Early modern and Elizabethan, 1500-1600 *(Collections, PR1262-3; History, PR646-658)*
  xx Historical drama
- — 17th century
- — Restoration, 1660-1700 *(Collections, PR1265-6; History, PR691-8)*
- — 18th century *(Collections, PR1269; History, PR701-719)*
- — 19th century *(Collections, PR1271; History, PR721-734)*
- — 20th century *(Collections, PR1272; History, PR736-9)*
- — African authors
  See African drama (English)
- — Caribbean authors
  See Caribbean drama (English)
- — East African authors
  See East African drama (English)
- — Guyanese authors
  See Guyanese drama
- — Indic authors
  See Indic drama (English)
- — Irish authors *(Collections, PR8864-8870; History, PR8783-8795)*
  x Irish drama (English)
- — Kenyan authors
  See Kenyan drama (English)
- — Malawian authors
  See Malawi drama (English)
- — Outlines, syllabi, etc.
  See English literature—Outlines, syllabi, etc.
- — Papua New Guinea authors
  See Papua New Guinea drama (English)
  Note under Welsh drama
- — West Indian authors
  See West Indian drama (English)
- — Zambian authors
  See Zambian drama (English)

  GEOGRAPHIC SUBDIVISIONS

- — Philippines
  See Philippine drama (English)
- — South Africa
  See South African drama (English)
English drama (Comedy) *(Collections, PR1248; History, PR631)*
- *sa* Ballad opera

Fig. 9. *Library of Congress Subject Headings* 1: 1039.

English literature *(Indirect)* *(Collections, PR1101-1149)*
- *sa* British literature
  Children's literature, English
  College readers
  Dialect literature, English
  Didactic literature, English
  Epic literature, English
  Fantastic literature, English
  Folk literature, English
  Laboring class writings, English
  Pastoral literature, English
- *xx* British literature
  Example under Anthologies; Authors; Germanic literature; Germanic philology
  Note under British literature
- — To 1100
  See Anglo-Saxon literature
- — Middle English, 1100-1500 *(Collections, PR1119-1131; History, PR251-369)*
  sa Romances, English
  Sermons, English—Middle English, 1100-1500
  x Middle English
  Old English literature
- — — Modernized versions
- — Early modern, 1500-1700 *(Collections, PR1119-1131; History, PR401-439)*
- — 18th century *(Collections, PR1134-9; History, PR441-9)*
- — 19th century *(Collections, PR1143-5; History, PR451-469)*
  x Literature, Victorian
  Victorian literature
- — 20th century *(Collections, PR1149; History, PR471-9)*
  sa Bloomsbury group
- — Abstracts
  See English literature—History and criticism—Abstracts
- — Adaptations
  sa English literature—Film and video adaptations
  x English literature—Paraphrases, tales, etc.
  Example under Literature—Adaptations

Fig. 10. *Library of Congress Subject Headings* 1: 1047.

You might, of course, use one or both of the last two headings, depending on the literary period you wish to study. The Library of Congress does have the subject heading "Stereotypes," although most of the books cataloged under that heading are sociological or psychological studies. You might even check for a general bibliography under these headings, looking for a card with the added subdivision "—Bibliography." Obviously, you would search as well under the names of the authors whose works you wish to discuss. The subdivision "—Characters" might also follow an author's name.

One further note about the catalog may be helpful. In January 1981, the Library of Congress changed its rules for cataloging books. Most libraries in the United States adopted the changes, which require listing some books according to a scheme that differs from the earlier one. For example, in the old system, books published with a pseudonym appeared in the card catalog under the author's real name. Now these books are listed under the pseudonym. So books by Mark Twain, which were in the catalog under "Clemens, Samuel Langhorne, 1835–1910," show up under "Twain, Mark, 1835–1910." While there will probably also be a Clemens card cross-referenced to Twain, you will not necessarily find such cross-referencing for less prominent authors.

As you might imagine, the new cataloging system has created some problems. How does a library integrate two incompatible sets of rules so that researchers can still find everything they need? Some libraries have decided simply to "close" the card catalog that uses the old rules and to start another for all books classified according to the new rules. If your library has chosen this course, you must consult both catalogs, old and new. Other libraries have decided to make all entries conform to the new rules, so that all books by the same author are together under one heading in one card catalog. In this system, for example, all the Samuel Clemens entries have been changed to read "Twain, Mark, 1835–1910." (Though seemingly ideal, this solution proved too costly for many libraries.) Still other libraries have their post-1981 books on an online or microform catalog, leaving their pre-1981 books in the card catalog. Undoubtedly there are many more variations. It is important for you to know how your library has chosen to deal with the new rules. Without this knowledge, you might overlook valuable books for your research.

A final word specifically about online catalogs is also in order. On an automated catalog, you can look up the record for a book just as you would in a traditional card catalog, namely, by author, title, or a Library of Congress subject heading. Besides having these familiar access points, many online catalogs can locate a book by its call number, by a combination of the author's name and the book's title, or even by keywords from its title or subject headings. In addition, some computerized catalogs allow you to specify the language or the format (e.g., book, periodical, recording, or film) of the materials that you are looking for. When you are generating a bibliography from an online catalog, you can even link several keywords by one of the so-called Boolean operators (*and*, *or*, or *not*) in order to contract or expand the number of "hits" in the data base. Using these features, you can conduct a more specific and refined search of the library's collection. This procedure can be especially valuable if you are confronted by a large university library with extensive holdings, by a total or partial lack of bibliographic information on a particular publication, or by errors in some bibliographic entries. Such errors happen far more frequently than one would wish.

Some libraries have designed their own online catalogs, while others have purchased hardware and software from companies that specialize in library automation services. Hence the specific characteristics of an online catalog can differ wildly from library to library. But clearly you need to become proficient in the use of the computerized catalog your library has.

Be sure to confer with your reference librarian before you finish this step in your research. The catalog is, quite obviously, an extremely powerful research tool, one to which you will often return as you work on your term paper. Incidently, keep track of the subject headings that you find in the catalog. Many of them are also used by the standard indexes discussed in the next two chapters.

3.
Finding Parts of Books

A subject heading in the card or online catalog directs you only to books that focus primarily or entirely on that subject. But some essays or chapters in books may pertain directly to your term-paper topic even though the over-all subject of the book may be far too broad for the catalog card to reflect this material. For example, a study of Keats's "To Autumn" may appear in a collection of essays on poetry in general or in a book on aesthetic the-ories that includes a chapter on Keats's ideas. Books of this sort are not listed in the catalog under "Keats, John, 1795–1821," because they are not predominantly about Keats or his works.

The *Essay and General Literature Index*, published since 1934, cites essays and chapters in such books in the humanities, social sciences, and natural sciences. Though far from comprehensive, it can direct you to discussions of specific subjects that are buried in more general collections. Issued twice a year, this index is cumulated first annually and then every five years. Liter-ary criticism is listed below an author's name under the subdivision "About individual works."

For example, in the 1980–84 cumulated volume of the *Essay and General Literature Index*, two essays on "To Autumn" are separated from the general criticism on Keats as well as from criticism on his other poems (fig. 11). The first of these, " 'To Autumn' and the Sound of Being," by Paul H. Fry, appears in Fry's book *The Poet's Calling in the English Ode* on pages 258–74. A list at the back of the guide provides full bibliographic information for the books indexed in that volume (fig. 12).

You should notice that the pages cited refer to full chapters, not to the part of a chapter that deals with a particular work. Thus Rajan's sixty-page chapter in *Dark Interpreter* is cited for two of Keats's poems, "Hyperion" and "The Fall of Hyperion" (fig. 11). How much of that chapter is devoted to either poem is impossible to determine from the index entry.

The *Essay and General Literature Index* is one of the few current guides that separate criticism on individual works from the larger body of general liter-ary criticism on an author. It is especially useful for criticism on individual poems, short stories, and other works that are not likely to have been cov-ered by a whole book.

Keats, John, 1795-1821—About—*Continued*
Meller, A. K. Keats and the vale of soul-making. *In* Meller, A. K. English romantic irony p77-108
Rajan, T. On the threshold of tragedy: Keat's late romances. *In* Rajan, T. Dark interpreter p97-142
Van Den Berg, S. S. Describing sonnets by Milton and Keats: Roy Schafer's action language and the interpretation of texts. *In* Psychological perspectives on literature: Freudian dissidents and non-Freudians, ed. by J. P. Natoli p134-54

About individual works

Endymion

Schapiro, B. A. Keats. *In* Schapiro, B. A. The romantic mother p33-60
Twitchell, J. B. Keats and Cozens: the systematic sublime. *In* Twitchell, J. B. Romantic horizons p136-62

The fall of Hyperion

Cantor, P. A. Romantic myth and tragic vision. *In* Cantor, P. A. Creature and creator p156-80
Rajan, T. Keats's Hyperion poems: the dialogue of Apollo and Dionysos. *In* Rajan, T. Dark interpreter p143-203
Schapiro, B. A. Keats. *In* Schapiro, B. A. The romantic mother p33-60

Hyperion

Cantor, P. A. Romantic myth and tragic vision. *In* Cantor, P. A. Creature and creator p156-80
Rajan, T. Keats's Hyperion poems: the dialogue of Apollo and Dionysos. *In* Rajan, T. Dark interpreter p143-203

Lamia

Rajan, T. On the threshold of tragedy: Keats's late romances. *In* Rajan, T. Dark interpreter p97-142
Skulsky, H. Lamia and the sophist: metamorphosis as the inexplicable. *In* Skulsky, H. Metamorphosis p148-70

On first looking into Chapman's Homer

Lipking, L. I. Beginning: a first look into Keats. *In* Kipking, L. I. The life of the poet p3-11

The poems of John Keats, ed. by Jack Stillinger

Jackson, D. H. Line indentation in Stillinger's The poems of John Keats. *In* Virginia. University. Bibliographical Society. Studies in bibliography v36 p200-05
Sharp, R. Stillinger's Keats. *In* Review v2 p127-36

To autumn

Fry, P. H. "To autumn" and the sound of being. *In* Fry, P. H. The poet's calling in the English ode p258-74
Vendler, H. H. Stevens and Keats' "To autumn." *In* Wallace Stevens, ed. by F. Doggett and R. Buttel p171-95

Fig. 11. *Essay and General Literature Index* 1980–84: 937.

ESSAY AND GENERAL LITERATURE INDEX, 1980-1984

Fry, Paul H. The poet's calling in the English ode. Yale Univ. Press 1980 328p ISBN 0-300-02400-2 LC 79-20554

Fry, Paul H. The reach of criticism; method and perception in literary theory. Yale Univ. Press 1983 239p ISBN 0-300-02924-1 LC 83-3535

Frye, Roland Mushat (ed.) Is God a creationist? The religious case against creation-science. *See* Is God a creationist? The religious case against creation-science

Fig. 12. *Essay and General Literature Index* 1980–84: 1980.

4.
Locating Articles in Periodicals

A great deal of literary criticism appears in scholarly journals rather than in books. For this reason, it is vital that you search for periodical articles on your topic. If you have found a good bibliography through the *Bibliographic Index* or the card or online catalog, you may already have citations for several journal articles. Then you need only consult your library's listing of periodical holdings to determine which are available (the reference librarian can help you use this tool). But even though you may locate some periodical articles through a bibliography for your topic, you should look for others in an appropriate index.

The *Humanities Index* is an excellent, up-to-date guide to current periodical articles in literature and the other humanities. It was formerly part of the *Social Sciences and Humanities Index*, which was once called the *International Index to Periodicals*. Covering nearly three hundred periodicals, it often has quite specific subject headings. For instance, although it does not use the narrower Library of Congress subject heading "Afro-Americans in literature," its alternative "Blacks in literature" not only yields a substantial list of periodical articles but also suggests other potentially helpful headings, such as "American literature — Black authors," "Black colleges and universities in literature," "Black theater," and "Black women in literature" (fig. 13). Each citation includes the title of the article, the author, a short form of the journal's name, volume and page numbers, and an abbreviation for the date of publication. The full names of the periodicals covered by the index are listed in the front of each volume (fig. 14). Thus you find that the article "The Images of Men in Lorraine Hansberry's Writing," by S. R. Carter, appears in the journal *Black American Literature Forum*, volume 19 (Winter 1985), pages 160–62.

H. W. Wilson, the publisher of the *Humanities Index*, offers electronic access to the more recent years of this index (since Feb. 1984) through two products, Wilsonline and Wilsondisc. The first is an online data-base retrieval system that the user plugs into over telecommunication lines through a microcomputer equipped with a modem. Wilsondisc, a CD–ROM version of the same data base, works on a microcomputer linked to a CD–ROM player. In most libraries, Wilsonline is searched by a librarian who, for a fee, works with the researcher to retrieve the citations needed. In contrast, Wilsondisc is usually made directly available to the library user, who can consult the data base without an intermediary and without charge.

Blacks in literature
> *See also*
> American literature—Black authors
> Black colleges and universities in literature
> Black theater
> Black women in literature
> Latin American literature—Black authors
> Mulattoes in literature
> Race relations in literature
> Slavery and slaves in literature
> West Indians in literature

Another look at Lawd today: Richard Wright's tricky apprenticeship. W. Burrison. *CLA J* 29:424-41 Je '86
Black culture in William Faulkner's That evening sun. D. Kuyk and others. bibl *J Am Stud* 20:33-50 Ap '86
Images of men in Lorraine Hansberry's writing. S. R. Carter. *Black Am Lit Forum* 19:160-2 Wint '85
The integration of Faulkner's Go down, Moses. J. Limon. *Crit Inq* 12:422-38 Wint '86

Fig. 13. *Humanities Index* 13: 97.

Ballet News — Ballet News
Biblic Archaeol — Biblical Archaeologist
Black Am Lit Forum — Black American Literature Forum
Br J Aesthet — The British Journal of Aesthetics
Br J Hist Sci — The British Journal for the History of Science
Br J Philos Sci — The British Journal for the Philosophy of Science
Bull Res Humanit — Bulletin of Research in the Humanities

Fig. 14. *Humanities Index* 13: xi.

A computerized search of either tool is normally faster and more efficient than a manual consultation of the printed version. Since the microcomputer, loaded with the appropriate software, enables you to search through the data base for a keyword or combination of keywords, you can more easily identify citations on topics too new or obscure to have subject headings in the printed versions. Similarly, the electronic versions of the *Humanities Index* permit you to sort out pertinent items from the plethora of citations for well-established authors. For example, a recent search of the Wilsonline data base found 997 entries for the subject "William Shakespeare," but by combining the terms *Hamlet* and *madness*, you could quickly locate the single study on madness in *Hamlet*: "Madness and Memory: Shakespeare's *Hamlet* and *King Lear*," published in the Summer 1985 issue of the journal *Comparative Drama* (fig. 15).

```
2/1    (HUM)
Madness and memory: Shakespeare's Hamlet and King Lear
Mazzaro, Jerome
Comparative Drama 19:97-116 Summ '85
Feature Article
Language: English
Subject heading: Memory in literature
Shakespeare, William
Shakespeare, William
Shakespeare, William
Special refs: Shakespeare, William/Plays/Hamlet
Special refs: Shakespeare, William/Plays/King Lear
Special refs: Shakespeare, William/Characters/Madmen
BHUM85024369
851016
Article
```

Fig. 15. Entry from *Humanities Index* on Wilsonline.

Whether you consult the printed *Humanities Index* or either of the computerized versions, the titles you find provide the only indication of the articles' relevance to your topic. There is no way to be absolutely certain that an article listed in the *Humanities Index* will be pertinent. One way around this problem is to consult *Abstracts of English Studies*, which serves as an index to a great range of periodicals and which also provides brief summaries (or abstracts) of the articles. The abstract is a common tool in the natural and the social sciences, but it is not so common in the humanities. *Abstracts of English Studies* is the only current compilation of abstracts for English and American literature.

From 1958, its first year of publication, through 1969, *Abstracts of English Studies* was arranged by the periodicals indexed. Under this system, major articles from each journal were cited and summarized with any others from that periodical, no matter how diverse the subjects. Since 1969, however, the abstracts have been organized chronologically by literary period and major author. A scant subject index to the citations is appended to each quarterly issue and cumulated into an annual list.

A portion of the subject index to *Abstracts of English Studies* shows the difficulties that can arise from this arrangement (fig. 16). Although entries for Shakespeare are subdivided by play, you must still turn to the front of the volume and check each number under *Hamlet* to determine which articles might be useful. The numbers indicate entries, not pages. Thus number 85-136 identifies Sara M. Deats's essay about kingship in *Hamlet*, which appears in the periodical *Essays in Literature*, volume 9, issue 1 (1982), pages 15–30 (fig. 17). Each abstract concludes with the initials of its author.

Despite its sketchy and cumbersome indexing, *Abstracts of English Studies* is undeniably useful. For limited research, it may be sufficient for your needs, although the *Humanities Index* is more likely to fill the bill.

Shakespeare, William	85-35, 122, 135-147, 155, 164, 177, 226, 250, 352, 444, 621, 722, 801, 802, 821, 860, 875, 877-921, 928-930, 958, 959, 978, 1026, 1031, 1142, 1551, 1650, 1654-1702, 1737, 1794, 1855, 1878, 1953, 2037, 2128, 2275, 2277, 2354, 2357, —c 2365-2375, 2377, 2415, 2646
All's Well	85-906
Antony	85-177, 444, 891, 1656, 2367
AYL	85-892, 903, 930, 1673
Errors	85-901
Cor.	85-142
Cym.	85-880, 894, 925, 930
Hamlet	85-136, 147, 802, 877, 883, 890, 902, 903, 916, 929, 959, 1645, 1666, 1670, 1671, 1697, 1701, 2365, 2366

Fig. 16. *Abstracts of English Studies* 28: 447.

William Shakespeare

85-135. Cox, John D. *The Medieval Background of MEASURE FOR MEASURE*, MP, 81, 1, 1983, 1-13. In *Measure* Shakespeare's treatment of sexual sin, the nature of kingship, and the contrast between the old Mosaic law and the new law of Christ echoes the treatment of these themes in medieval drama. Shakespeare need not have read such miracle plays as the Digby *Mary Magdalene* or the N-Town *Joseph's Return* to have been influenced by their dramaturgy. Such plays were performed in England through the mid 1580's and hence were directly accessible to the young Shakespeare. F.M.

85-136. Deats, Sara.M. *The Once and Future Kings: Four Studies of Kingship in HAMLET*, EIL, 9, 1, 1982, 15-30. King Hamlet provides the standard of kingship against which we may evaluate the actual kingship of Claudius and the potential kingship of Hamlet and Fortinbras. King Hamlet was a forceful and just ruler, evincing both public and private virtue, whereas Claudius is the stereotypic Machiavel and Fortinbras, a hot-headed bully. Prince Hamlet, although capable of ideal kingship, delays in accepting his public responsibilities and thus causes a state as well as a personal tragedy — bellicose Fortinbras on the throne. N.C.M.

Fig. 17. *Abstracts of English Studies* 28: 27.

5.
Using Annual Bibliographies

Because both the *Humanities Index* and *Abstracts of English Studies* are limited to a narrow range of periodicals, you often need to consult a source with broader coverage. The *MLA International Bibliography of Books and Articles on the Modern Languages and Literatures*, known as the *MLA Bibliography*, is just such a tool. It annually compiles books, periodical articles, doctoral dissertations, and essays in festschriften (collections of essays in honor of some person or some event) for the entire field of modern languages and literatures, not just English. From 1921 to 1955 the *MLA Bibliography* listed only literary criticism from the United States. But since 1955 it has become increasingly international in scope, currently indexing books and over three thousand periodicals published throughout the world.

The format of the *MLA Bibliography* has changed over the years. Since 1981 there have been five distinct sections for each annual list of criticism. The first section offers the classified listing for literatures in the English language (fig. 18). (Other sections deal with literatures in other language groups.) Notice that the numbers listed alongside each of these literatures designate entries, not pages. Within the subsection devoted to each of these literatures is a much finer breakdown — by literary period in chronological order, by author, and then by author's work. Thus criticism of *Hamlet* appears within the subsection on "English Literature" during the period "1500–1599," then under "Shakespeare, William (1564–1616)," and finally under "Tragedy/Hamlet (1600–1601)" (fig. 19).

The appropriate entries in the 1983 volume begin with number 1232 (fig. 19): "The Stamp of One Defect," written by Michael Cameron Andrews and published in the *Shakespeare Quarterly*, volume 34, issue 2 (1983), pages 217–18. The "Master List of Periodicals in Acronym Order," located in the front of each volume, provides the full title for the journal, abbreviated *SQ* in our example (fig. 20).

The *MLA Bibliography* lists books as well as periodical articles. In figure 19, item 1237 cites the book *To Be and Not to Be: Negation and Metadrama in Hamlet*, by James L. Calderwood, published by Columbia University Press. In addition to books and journal articles, the *MLA Bibliography* indexes both individual essays in collections and doctoral dissertations. Entry 1242, for example, "Shakespeare and Kyd," is an essay in the book *Shakespeare, Man of the Theater*, edited by Kenneth Muir and others. The 1983 volume lists several doctoral dissertations under "Shakespeare, William (1564–1616)/ Tragedy," including entry 1211, "The Representation of Suffering in Six of

The classification structure of the *MLA International Bibliography* accommodates all areas of literary study. This guide to the classified listings includes classification headings for literatures in the English language. The numbers following the headings refer to the first bibliographical entry number listed under a particular heading. Headings under which no books, articles, or other documents appear are omitted from this guide. Users wishing to locate documents on more specific topics or concepts are directed to the Subject Index that accompanies this volume.

Literatures of the British Isles	1	English-Caribbean Literature	6320
ENGLISH LITERATURE	6	BARBADIAN LITERATURE	6331
IRISH LITERATURE	4923	GUYANESE LITERATURE	6332
SCOTTISH LITERATURE	5640	JAMAICAN LITERATURE	6343
WELSH LITERATURE	5830	ST. LUCIAN LITERATURE	6346
		TRINIDAD AND TOBAGO LITERATURE	6350
British Commonwealth Literature	5893	New Zealand Literature	6362
AUSTRALIAN LITERATURE	5898		
CANADIAN LITERATURE	6111	American (U.S.A.) Literature	6369

Fig. 18. *1983 MLA International Bibliography of Books and Articles on the Modern Languages and Literatures* 1: "Guide to Classified Listings."

English literature/1500-1599
SHAKESPEARE, WILLIAM (1564-1616)/ *Tragedy · Julius Caesar (1599)*

[1231] Velz, John W. "Cracking Strong Curbs Asunder: Roman Destiny and the Roman Hero in *Coriolanus*." *ELR* 1983 Winter; 13(1): 58-69. [†Treatment of history; relationship to individualism. Sources in Virgil: *Aeneid*.]

Tragedy/Hamlet (1600-1601)

[1232] Andrews, Michael Cameron. "The Stamp of One Defect." *SQ* 1983 Summer; 34(2): 217-218.
[1233] Baldo, Jonathan. "'He That Plays the King': The Problem of Pretending in *Hamlet*." *Criticism*. 1983 Winter; 25(1): 13-26.
[1234] Ben-Zion, D. K. "Hamlet Ben Zmaneinu." *Iton* 77. 1983; 44-45: 72. [†Review article.]
[1235] Bennett, Robert B. "Hamlet and the Burden of Knowledge." *ShakS*. 1982; 15: 77-97. [†Treatment of knowledge. Sources in Christian humanism.]
[1236] Breuer, Horst. "Shakespeare's *Hamlet*, III.i.56-88." *Expl*. 1982 Spring; 40(3): 14-15.
[1237] Calderwood, James L. *To Be and Not to Be: Negation and Metadrama in* Hamlet. New York: Columbia UP; 1983. xvi, 222 pp. [†As metadrama. Treatment of negation; contradiction; paradox.]
[1238] Cohen, Eileen Z. "*Hamlet* and *The Murder of Gonzago*: Two Perspectives." *RBPH*. 1983; 3: 543-556.
[1239] Coyle, Martin. "Shakespeare's *Hamlet*." *Expl*. 1982 Spring; 40(3): 13.
[1240] Des Jardins, Gregory. "The Hyrcanian Beast." *N&Q* 1983 Apr.; 30 [228](2): 124-125.
[1241] Draudt, Manfred. "Another Senecan Echo in *Hamlet*." *SQ*. 1983 Summer; 34(2): 216-217. [†Sources in Seneca.]
[1242] Edwards, Philip. "Shakespeare and Kyd." 148-154 in Muir, Kenneth, ed. & pref.; Halio, Jay L., ed.; Palmer, D. J., ed.; Schoenbaum, S[amuel], pref. *Shakespeare, Man of the Theater*. Newark: U of Delaware P; 1983. London: Associated UPs; 1983. 265 pp. [†Compared to *Julius Caesar* as political drama. Treatment of ghost compared to Kyd, Thomas: *The Spanish Tragedy*.]

[1260] Nardo, Anna K. "Hamlet, 'A Man to Double Business Bound'." *SQ* 1983 Summer; 34(2): 181-199.
[1261] Newman, Karen. "Hayman's Missing *Hamlet*." *SQ* 1983 Spring; 34(1): 73-78. [†On illustration by Hayman, Francis.]
[1262] Oakes, Elizabeth Thompson. "'Killing the Calf' in *Hamlet*." *SQ*. 1983 Summer; 34(2): 215-216.
[1263] Pfister, Manfred. "Moderne Hamlet-Bearbeitungen im Spannungsfeld aktueller Dramaturgien." I: 953-984 in Ahrens, Rüdiger, ed. *William Shakespeare: Didaktisches Handbuch, Band 1*. Munich: Fink, 1982. 1099 pp. (Uni-Taschenbücher 1111-1113.) [†On dramatic adaptation. Pedagogical approach.]
[1264] Pistotnik, Vesna. "Teatar ITD's Hamlet." *HSt*. 1982 Summer-Winter; 4(1-2): 95-98. [†On theatrical production in Yugoslavia: Zagreb (1982) by Teatar ITD.]
[1265] Ronan, Clifford J. "*Homo Multiplex* and the 'Man' Equivocation in *Hamlet*." *HSt*. 1982 Summer-Winter; 4(1-2): 33-53.
[1266] Shaheen, Naseeb. "*A Warning for Fair Women* and the *Ur-Hamlet*." *N&Q*. 1983 Apr.; 30 [228](2): 126-127. [†Sources in *A Warning for Faire Women*; relationship to Kyd, Thomas: *The Spanish Tragedy*.]
[1267] Smith, Gordon Ross. "The McCarter Theatre Company's *Hamlet*." *HSt*. 1982 Summer-Winter; 4(1-2): 106-108. [†On theatrical production (1982) by McCarther Theatre Company.]
[1268] Sternlicht, Sanford. "Hamlet: The Actor as Prince." *HSt*. 1982 Summer-Winter; 4(1-2): 19-32.
[1269] Sugiyama, Shigeo. "Hamlet and the Ghost." *SELit*. 1982 Sept.; 59(1): 17-27. [In Japanese; Eng. sum. in 1983; 59(Eng. no.): 250-251.]
[1270] Suhamy, Henri. "The Metaphorical Fallacy: Some Remarks on the Sickness Imagery in *Hamlet*." *CahiersE*. 1983 Oct.; 24: 27-32.
[1271] Taylor, Gary. "The Folio Copy for *Hamlet*, *King Lear*, and *Othello*." *SQ*. 1983 Spring; 34(1): 44-61. [†*King Lear*; *Othello*. Textual criticism; role of compositor. Theories of Hinman, Charlton; Howard-Hill, T. H.]
[1272] Tobin, J. J. M. "'Bawds' not 'Bonds'." *HSt*. 1982 Summer-Winter; 4(1-2): 93-95. [†Sources in Apuleius: *Metamorphoses*.]

Fig. 19. *1983 MLA Bibliography* 1: 33.

Spsp Sprachspiegel: Schweizerische Zeitschrift für die deutsche Muttersprache
SPsy Social Psychology Quarterly
* *SPWVSRA* Selected Papers from the West Virginia Shakespeare and Renaissance Association
* *SQ* Shakespeare Quarterly
* *SR* Sewanee Review
* *SRC* Studies in Religion/Sciences Religieuses: Revue Canadienne/A Canadian Journal
SRev The Sayers Review
* *SRIELA* Selected Reports in Ethnomusicology
* *SRL* Studies in Romance Languages
SRLing Studia Romanica et Linguistica

Fig. 20. *1983 MLA Bibliography* 1: xxxvi.

Shakespeare's Tragedies," by Jill O'Hora Geare (fig. 21). As explained in the acronyms list, the abbreviation *DAI* stands for *Dissertations Abstracts International*, which provides brief summaries of doctoral dissertations. (You are probably unlikely to locate a copy of the dissertation itself, unless it was written by a doctoral student at your university. Libraries rarely acquire dissertations submitted at other institutions.)

Since 1981 the *MLA* has also published a separate subject index that complements the classified sections. For topics like the stereotypical characterization of blacks in American literature, the subject index proves indispensable. For your research on this topic, you might look in the 1983 subject index under the heading "Afro-Americans" (fig. 22). The first entry leads to an appropriate article on Herman Melville's *Benito Cereno*. Full bibliographic information can be found in the American literature subsection of volume 1, item 7342: "The Topicality of Depravity in 'Benito Cereno,'" by Allan Moore Emery (fig. 23).

To conduct a thorough search of the post-1980 *MLA Bibliography*, always consult the subject index, even though you can turn directly to the classi-

---

Tragedy

[1208] Bodin, Per-Arne, tr. "Anteckningar till översättningarna av Shakespeares tragedier." *Artes*. 1983; 1: 80-98. [†On Russian language translation by Pasternak, Boris Leonidovich.]

[1209] Brockbank, Philip. "Blood and Wine: Tragic Ritual from Aeschylus to Soyinka." *ShS*. 1983; 36: 11-19. [†Relationship to Soyinka, Wole.]

[1210] Bushnell, Rebecca Weld. "The Defiance of Augury: The Hero and Prophet in Sophoclean and Shakespearean Tragedy." *DAI*. 1983 Mar.; 43(9): 2988A. [†Treatment of augury compared to Sophocles. Dissertation abstract.]

[1211] Geare, Jill O'Hora. "The Representation of Suffering in Six of Shakespeare's Tragedies." *DAI*. 1983 Sept.; 44(3): 758A. [†Treatment of anguish. Dissertation abstract.]

[1212] Polgar, Mirko. "Šekspir i 'natprirodne' sile." *Savremenik*. 1980 Jan.-Feb.; 51(1-2): 22-45. [†Treatment of the supernatural.]

Fig. 21. *1983 MLA Bibliography* 1: 32.

AFRO-AMERICANS
See also related term: Black life.

American literature. Fiction. 1800-1899.
Melville, Herman. *Benito Cereno*. Treatment of AFRO-AMERICANS; slavery; depravity. Sources in Delano, Amasa: *A Narrative of Voyages and Travels, in the Northern and Southern Hemispheres*. 1:7342.

American literature. Film and television. 1900-1999.
Treatment of AFRO-AMERICANS; relationship to race relations. 1:7718.

Fig. 22. *1983 MLA Bibliography* G25.

Fiction/Benito Cereno

[7342] Emery, Allan Moore. "The Topicality of Depravity in 'Benito Cereno'." *AL*. 1983 Oct.; 55(3): 316-331. [†Treatment of Afro-Americans; slavery; depravity. Sources in Delano, Amasa: *A Narrative of Voyages and Travels, in the Northern and Southern Hemispheres*.]
[7343] Fulcher, James. "Melville's 'Benito Cereno': An American Mystery." *Clues*. 1981 Spring-Summer; 2(1): 116-122. [†Plot. Sources in detective fiction; especially Poe, Edgar Allan.]
[7344] Leslie, Joshua; Stuckey, Sterling. "The Death of Benito Cereno: A Reading of Herman Melville on Slavery." *JNH*. 1982 Winter; 67(4): 287-301. [†Sources in Park, Mungo: *Travels in the Interior Districts of Africa*.]

Fig. 23. *1983 MLA Bibliography* 1: 203.

fied listing of criticism on specific authors and literary works. Any given article, book, or other publication is listed only once in the classified sections. In other words, a critical study that compares works by two or more authors shows up in the bibliography under the name of just one of those authors. Pick the wrong author and you miss the citation, unless you consult the subject index for cross-references to other pertinent entries. If you don't use this index, for instance, you will probably overlook a book about the Romantic period that contains an inspired insight into Keats's "To Autumn."

Under the format for the *MLA Bibliography* between 1968 and 1980, each annual edition has three distinct sections or volumes, and there is no subject index. For example, if you turn to the table of contents for the first section of the 1978 edition, which lists criticism on English and American authors (fig. 24), you will notice that it is a bit more detailed than the "Guide to Classified Listings" in the post-1980 editions. Since there is no separate subject indexing for the 1968–80 editions, the table of contents is your only guide to the part of the volume devoted to your topic. Criticism of Keats's poetry appears under "ENGLISH LITERATURE IX. Nineteenth Cen-

TABLE OF CONTENTS
VOLUME I

Guide for Users of the 1978 *Bibliography*	v	ENGLISH LITERATURE	
		I. General and Miscellaneous	2218
Master List of Periodicals in Acronym Order	xiv	II. Australia, Canada, etc.	2234
Master List of Periodicals in Title Order	xliv	III. Themes, Types, and Special Topics	3021
Author Index	313	IV. Old English	3068
		Beowulf	3122
	Item	V. Middle English	3199
		Chaucer	3434
Festschriften and Other Analyzed Collections	1	VI. Renaissance and Elizabethan	3572
GENERAL LITERATURE AND		Shakespeare	3937
RELATED TOPICS		VII. Seventeenth Century	4471
I. Esthetics	250	Milton	4878
II. Literary Criticism and Literary Theory	340	VIII. Eighteenth Century	5070
III. Literature, General and Comparative	892	IX. Nineteenth Century	5660
IV. Themes and Types	1134	X. Twentieth Century	7031
V. Bibliographical	2097		
VI. Miscellaneous	2129		

Fig. 24. *1978 MLA Bibliography* 1: iii

tury," a division that begins with item 5660. Citations for individual authors follow the "General and Miscellaneous" portion of each literary period. In the 1978 volume, entries specifically devoted to Keats begin with the number 6560 (fig. 25). For most citations, the title of the work is your only clue to the subject matter and its applicability to your research needs. Perusing the entire section devoted to Keats, you must wade through close to forty citations to find just two that clearly discuss "To Autumn." Then, to check the relevance of other criticism that deals with Keats, you must flip back and forth in the volume, tracking down the fourteen "see also" entries (fig. 25). All in all, the MLA made a wise decision when it changed the bibliography's format in 1981.

While consulting the 1968–80 volumes, you may come upon citations from collections of essays that were analyzed by the editors of the *MLA Bibliography*. An example is entry number 6598 in figure 25. Following the list of periodical abbreviations in the front of each volume is a numbered list of festschriften and other analyzed collections (fig. 26). Aileen Ward's " 'That Last Infirmity of Nobel Mind': Keats and the Idea of Fame" is on pages 312–33 in collection 111, which turns out to be *The Evidence of the Imagination: Studies of Interactions between Life and Art in English Romantic Literature*, edited by Donald H. Reiman and others. Since 1981, the *MLA Bibliography* has dispensed with the separate list of festschriften; it now simply includes the full bibliographic information in each citation.

As you read through the entries in the *MLA Bibliography*, you may have noticed that some titles are in foreign languages. This bibliography is intended to be international in scope, so that you can expect to find criticism of English and American authors that has been published in foreign language journals or by foreign language publishers.

The printed version of the *MLA Bibliography* has some disadvantages. The year's delay in publication makes it less current than the quarterly *Humanities Index*, and conducting a search on a thematic topic can be very difficult when you use volumes before 1981 and the advent of subject indexing. Given a subject like the stereotyping of blacks in American fiction, you would have to specify certain authors before examining the pre-1981 editions. You can avoid both these difficulties by using one of the electronic versions of the *MLA Bibliography*.

Electronic coverage of the bibliography begins with the 1981 volume, through Wilsonline online and Wilsondisc on CD–ROM, both discussed in the previous chapter. Listings since 1964 are also available on an online retrieval service called Dialog. In searching in these electronic versions of the bibliography, you can again use the Boolean operators — *and*, *or*, and *not* — to define subjects narrowly or broadly. On Wilsondisc, we can try the same strategy in the *MLA Bibliography* as we did in the *Humanities Index*. Linking the terms *Hamlet* and *madness* with the Boolean operator *and* turned up one

Keats. 6560. Akikuni, Tadanori. "The Ambiguity of Eternity: An Essay on the Theme and Structure of the 'Ode on a Grecian Urn'." *SELit* 55:31-44. [In Jap.]

6561. Brown, Keith. "A Short *Course of the Belles Lettres* for Keatsians?" *English* 27:27-32. ["Ode on a Grecian Urn."]

6562. Bush, Douglas. "The Milton of Keats and Arnold." *MiltonS* 11:99-114.

6563. Candido, Joseph. "*A Midsummer Night's Dream* and 'Ode to a Nightingale': A Further Instance of Keats's Indebtedness." *AN&Q* 16:154-55.

6564. Curtis, Marcia Smith. "John Keats's Gordian Imagination." *DAI* 39:1583A.

6565. Flautz, John. "On Most Recently Looking into 'On First Looking into Chapman's Homer'." *CEA* 40,iii:24-27.

6566. Flick, A. J. "Keats's First Reading of Dante's *Divine Comedy*." *N&Q* 25:225.

6567. Freeman, Donald C. "Keats's 'To Autumn': Poetry as Process and Pattern." *Lang&S* 11:3-17.

6568. Garrett, William. "The Glaucus Episode: An Interpretation of Book III of *Endymion*." *KSJ* 27:23-34.

6569. Gleckner, Robert F. "Keats's 'How Many Bards' and Poetic Tradition." *KSJ* 27:14-22.

6570. Hajevs'kyj, C. "*Vybrani poeziji* Džona Kitsa." [F 126] 353-54. [Yar Slavutych's Ukr. tr. of Keats.]

6571. Harris, Irene Strickler. "The Influence of Shakespeare on the Odes of Keats." *DAI* 38:7345A.

6572. Hill, James L. "The Function of the Poem in Keats's 'Ode on a Grecian Urn' and Wordsworth's 'Resolution and Independence'." *CentR* 22:424-44.

6573. Jones, Leonidas M. "The Date of 'Lines on the Mermaid Tavern'." *ELN* 15:186-88.

6574. Jones, Stanley. "A Glimpse of George Keats in Philadelphia." *KSMB* 28(1977):29-31.

6575. Kappel, Andrew J. "The Immortality of the Natural: Keats' 'Ode to a Nightingale'." *ELH* 45:270-79, 282-84.

6576. Kōmoto, Yōko. "Keats and Reality." *AnRS* 28(1977):118-40. [In Jap.]

6577. Kostec'kyj, I. "Džon Kits: *Vybrani poeziji*." [F 126] 349-53. [Yar Slavutych's Ukr. tr. of Keats.]

6578. Kramer, Lawrence. "The Return of the Gods: Keats to Rilke." *SIR* 17:483-500.

6579. Luke, David. "Keats's Letters: Fragments of an Aesthetic of Fragments." *Genre* 11:209-26.

6580. Matsushita, Senkichi. "On the Delicately Equipoised Harmony between Carnality and Spirituality of Love: Notes on the 'Ode to Psyche'." *SELit* 55:45-59. [In Jap.]

6581. Mizunoe, Yuichi. *Sapience: The Philosophy of John Keats*. Tokyo: Shohakusha. 202 pp.

6582. Morsberger, Robert E. "Keats vs. Coleridge on Negative Capability." *Par Rapport* (Marshall, MN) 1:132-38.

6583. Nemoianu, Virgil. "The Dialectics of Movement in Keats's 'To Autumn'." *PMLA* 93:205-14.

6584. Ogawa, Kazuo. "*Ode on Melancholy* Chukai." *EigoS* 123:434-47, 520-23, 565-68; 124:17-19, 50-52.

6585. ——. "*Ode to Psyche* Chukai." *EigoS* 124:290-94, 472-76, 529-33 (to be cont.).

6586. Priest, Dale G. "Void and Vision in Keats' Poetry." *LJHum* 4,ii:42-54.

6587. Pulsiano, Phillip J. " 'Things All Disjointed': Keats's 'Epistle to J.H. Reynolds'." *GyS* 5:96-101.

6588. Richards, Bernard. "Keats and the Lives of the Cat." *N&Q* 25:225.

6589. Rooke, Constance. "Romance and Reality in The Eve of St. Agnes." *ESC* 4:25-40.

6590. Sherwin, Paul. "Dying into Life: Keats's Struggle with Milton in *Hyperion*." *PMLA* 93:383-95.

6591. Spiegelman, Willard. "Another Shakespearean Echo in Keats." *AN&Q* 17:3-4.

6592. Stillinger, Jack, ed. *The Poems of John Keats*. Cambridge: Harvard UP. 769 pp.

6593. Swinden, Patrick. "John Keats: 'To Autumn'." *CritQ* 20,iv:57-60.

6594. Taylor, Mark. "Keats' 'Ode to a Nightingale'." *Expl* 36,iii:24-26.

6595. Twitchell, James B. "Porphyro as 'Famish'd Pilgrim': The Hoodwinking of Madeline Continued." *BSUF* 19,ii:56-65. [See 1961 Bibliog. 3947.]

6596. Vaillancourt, Andre Philippe. "John Keats' Dissolving Imagination: Its Paradisal and Demonic Dimensions." *DAI* 38:7352A.

6597. Verghese, P. C. "A Worshipper of Beauty." *ComQ* 2,vii:124-27.

6598. Ward, Aileen. " 'That Last Infirmity of Nobel Mind': Keats and the Idea of Fame." [F 111] 312-33.

6599. Wooster, Margaret Irene. "Against Closure: Keats and the Suspense of Writing." *DAI* 39:302A.

See also 1772, 4384, 5662, 5664, 5724, 5728, 5759, 5971, 6029, 6812, 6970, 7883, 8581, 11749.

Fig. 25. *1978 MLA Bibliography* 1: 126–27.

109. Quinn, Edward, ed. *How to Read Shakespearean Tragedy*. New York: Harper. 402 pp. [Pref. ix-xii; "Shakespeare: An Introduction," 1-32.]

110. *Recent Research on Ben Jonson*. (JDS 76.) Salzburg: Inst. für eng. Sprache & Lit., Univ. Salzburg. 136 pp.

111. Reiman, Donald H., Michael C. Jaye, Betty T. Bennett, Doucet Devin Fischer, & Ricki B. Herzfeld, eds. *The Evidence of the Imagination: Studies of Interactions between Life and Art in English Romantic Literature*. (Gotham Lib.) New York: New York UP. 409 pp. [Foreword Carl H. Pforzheimer, Jr., ix-x; introd., xiii-xvii.]

112. [Richardson, David A., ed.] *Spenser at Kalamazoo*. Proc. from a Spec. Session at the 13th Conference on Medieval Studies in Kalamazoo, Michigan, 5-6 May 1978. Cleveland:

Fig. 26. *1978 MLA Bibliography* 1: 4.

```
1 MLA
Vey-Miller, Marguerite M. Miller, Ronald J.
Degrees of Psychopathology in Hamlet
Hamlet Studies: An International Journal of Research on The
Tragedie of Hamlet, Prince of Denmarke 1985 Summer-Winter 7(1-2):
81-87

SUBJECTS COVERED:
--(slt) English literature (tim) 1500-1599 (sau) Shakespeare,
William (swk) Hamlet/tragedy (lth) madness


2 MLA
Analytic
Showalter, Elaine

Representing Ophelia: Women, Madness, and the Responsibilities
of Feminist Criticism 77-94 IN Parker, Patricia (ed.) Hartman,
Geoffrey (ed.) Shakespeare and the Question of Theory. New York:
Methuen: 1985. xiii, 335 pp.

SUBJECTS COVERED:
--(slt) English literature (tim) 1500-1599 (sau) Shakespeare,
William (swk) Hamlet/tragedy (lth) madness (lth) sexuality (lth)
Ophelia (character) (lth) painting (lth) theatrical production
(lth) psychoanalytic literature (lth) feminist criticism (sap)
feminist approach


3 MLA
Analytic
Davidson, Hilda R. Ellis

The Hero as a Fool: The Northern Hamlet : Papers Read at Conf.
of Folklore Soc. Held at Dyffryn House, Cardiff, July 1982 30-45
IN Davidson, Hilda R. Ellis (ed.) Blacker, Carmen (introd.) The
Hero in Tradition and Folklore. London: Folklore Soc.; 1984. x,
183 pp.

SUBJECTS COVERED:
--(slt) English literature (tim) 1500-1599 (sau) Shakespeare,
William (swk) Hamlet/tragedy (sau) Ariosto, Ludovico (swk)
Orlando furioso (sau) Cervantes Saavedra, Miguel de (swk) Quijote
(sau) Dostoevskii, Fedor Mikhailovich (swk) Idiot (lth) hero
(lth) fool
3    (MLA)    continued...
--(slt) Italian literature/poetry
--(lfe) fool (lth) themes and figures/400-1899 (lso) Celtic
folklore (lso) Germanic folklore
--(loc) Scandinavia (loc) Germany/400-1499 (gen) folk literature
(gen) folk narrative (gen) legend (lth) madness (lth) Old Norse
literature


4 MLA
Mazzaro, Jerome
Madness and Memory: Shakespeare's Hamlet and King Lear
Comparative Drama 1985 Summer 19(2): 97-116

SUBJECTS COVERED:
--(slt) English literature (tim) 1500-1599 (sau) Shakespeare,
William (swk) Hamlet (swk) King Lear/tragedy (lth) madness (lth)
memory


5 MLA
Bentley, Greg
Melancholy, Madness and Syphilis in Hamlet
Hamlet Studies: An International Journal of Research on The
Tragedie of Hamlet, Prince of Denmarke 1984 Summer-Winter 6(1-2):
75-80

SUBJECTS COVERED:
--(slt) English literature (tim) 1500-1599 (sau) Shakespeare,
William (swk) Hamlet/tragedy (lth) melancholy (lth) madness (lth)
syphilis


6 MLA
Hallett, Charles A. Hallett, Elaine S.
The Revenger's Madness: A Study of Revenge Tragedy Motifs
U of Nebraska P 1980 349 pp.

SUBJECTS COVERED:
--(slt) English literature (tim) 1500-1699 (sau) Kyd, Thomas
(swk) The Spanish Tragedy (sau) Marston, John (swk) Antonio's
Revenge (sau) Tourneur, Cyril (swk) Revenger's Tragedy (sau)
Shakespeare, William (swk) Hamlet (gen) drama (gen) revenge
tragedy


7 MLA
Proser, Matthew N.
Madness, Revenge, and the Metaphor of the Theater in
Shakespeare's Hamlet and Pirandello's Henry IV
Modern Drama 1981 Sept. 24(3): 338-352

SUBJECTS COVERED:
--(slt) English literature (tim) 1500-1599 (sau) Shakespeare,
William (swk) Hamlet/tragedy (sau) Pirandello, Luigi (swk) Enrico
IV (ltc) metaphor (lth) theater (lth) madness (lth) revenge
--(slt) Italian literature (tim) 1900-1999/drama
```

Fig. 27. From *MLA Bibliography* on Wilsondisc.

citation in the *Humanities Index*, but the *MLA Bibliography* search quickly sorts out, from all the other literary criticism on Shakespeare, a neat and convenient list — seven entries dealing with madness in *Hamlet* (fig. 27). Each citation indicates the "SUBJECTS COVERED," and looking up some of these terms might yield other useful materials.

As I said earlier, the subject indexes for the *MLA Bibliography* are indispensable for finding criticism relevant to a general topic like stereotypical blacks in American literature. Computerized versions of the bibliography offer even more power for such searches. Thus, when you combine the three concepts *blacks*, *American literature*, and *stereotypes* online with Wilsondisc, the computer culls six items from the enormous body of criticism on American literature cited in seven years of the *MLA Bibliography*. These entries are shown in figure 28. Because it covers the bibliography since 1964, Dialog would have produced even more citations in the same search.

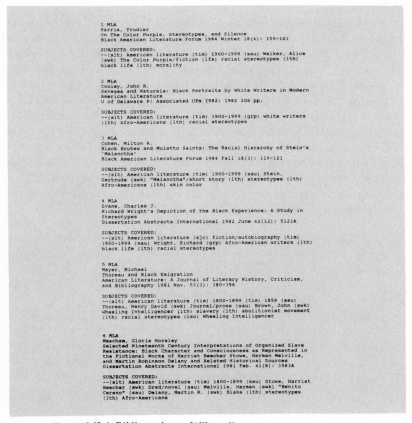

Fig. 28. From *MLA Bibliography* on Wilsondisc.

To conduct effective electronic searches, you must remember that computers are literal about the English language. If you ask for the term *blacks*, the computer may not automatically look under alternative terms such as *Afro-Americans*. Singular or plural forms of nouns can also cause the computer to miss entries. To put together the bibliography on the stereotyping of blacks in American literature, Wilsonline needed to key on the following terms: *black* or *blacks* or *Afro-American* or *Afro-Americans* or *Negro* or *negroes*; and *stereotype* or *stereotypes*; and *American literature*. If you had asked for only one of the synonyms for *blacks*, Wilsonline would have missed some of the twelve items derived from the search. Some electronic indexes use Library of Congress subject headings; others are free-text, indexing from keywords in the titles of the entries. Librarians who consult Wilsonline and Dialog for you are trained to anticipate these and other pitfalls. If your library offers self-service access to these online systems or to Wilsondisc, you will need some preliminary instruction or some practice before you can perform reliable searches.

The *Annual Bibliography of English Language and Literature* (*ABELL*) is the British equivalent of the first section of the *MLA Bibliography*. Like its American counterpart, *ABELL* provides citations for books, articles in periodicals, essays in collections, and dissertations on English and American literature and languages. While both annual bibliographies are international in coverage, *ABELL* is less complicated to use. Each volume of *ABELL* is also arranged by literary period and then by author, but in the back of the volume an index for authors, subjects, and critics leads you directly to the entries on your topic. The Keats citations in the *ABELL* volume for 1977 begin with item 7381 and end with 7419 (fig. 29). Entry 7405 is a discussion of "To Autumn" (fig. 30). Note that *ABELL* gives the volume number for a journal in parentheses. A list of abbreviations appears in the front of each volume.

Kaufman, George S., 10802–3
Kavanagh, Patrick, 10804–5
Keats, John, 7381–419
Kelley, William Melvin, 10806
Kelly, Hugh, 5572
Keneally, Thomas, 10807–12
Kennedy, John Pendleton, 7420
Kerouac, Jack, 10813–18
Kesey, Ken, 10819–25
Kiely, Benedict, 10826
Killens, John Oliver, 10827
Kilroy, Thomas, 10828
King, Clarence, 7421–2
— Stephen, 10829
Kingsley, Charles, 7423–5
— Henry, 7426
Kingsmill, Hugh, 10830–1

Fig. 29. *Annual Bibliography of English Language and Literature* 1977: 696.

One special feature of *ABELL* is its coverage of book reviews. Figure 30, for example, indicates that the journal *English Studies* has reviewed Christopher Ricks's *Keats and Embarrassment* (which, according to the parenthetical note, was entry 8858 in the 1976 volume of *ABELL*). Reviews can give you some idea of how a book of criticism has been evaluated by literary scholars and help you assess its usefulness.

7396. JONES, LEONIDAS M. Keats's favorite play. ELN (15) 43–4. ('Antony and Cleopatra'.)
7397. KAZIN, ALFRED. Rome: a meditation on Keats. ASch (46) 1976/77, 109–15.
7398. KING, E. H. Beattie and Keats: the progress of the Romantic minstrel. *See* **5169.**
7399. LANGE, DONALD. A new Reynolds–Milnes letter: were there two meetings between Keats and Coleridge? *See* **6590.**
7400. LITTLE, JUDY. Keats as a narrative poet: a test of invention. Lincoln: Nebraska UP, 1975. pp. 167. Rev. by Brian Wilkie in KSJ (26) 145–6.
7401. MARQUARD, JEAN. Ideas and experience in 'Ode to a Nightingale'. Crux (11:2) 51–6.
7402. MARTIN, WILLIAM JOSEPH. John Keats and the aesthetics of the imagination. Unpub. doct. diss., Univ. of Notre Dame. [Abstr. in DA (38) 1413A.]
7403. MATTHEY, FRANÇOIS. The evolution of Keats's structural imagery. (Bibl. 1976, 8848.) Rev. by Arthur Clayborough in EngS (58) 360–4.
7404. PARSONS, COLEMAN O. Primitive sense in 'Lamia'. *See* **2144.**
7405. PEARCE, DONALD. Thoughts on the Autumn Ode of Keats. Ariel (6:3) 1975, 3–19.
7406. PISON, THOMAS. A phenomenological approach to Keats's 'To Autumn'. BuR (22:1) 1976, 37–47.
7407. RAYAN, KRISHNA. The Grecian urn re-read. Mosaic (11:1) 15–20.
7408. RICKS, CHRISTOPHER. Keats and embarrassment. (Bibl. 1976, 8858.) Rev. by Arthur Clayborough in EngS (58) 68–74.
7409. RYAN, ROBERT M. Keats: the religious sense. (Bibl. 1976, 8864.) Rev. by Stuart M. Sperry in MLQ (38) 178–85.
7410. —— Keats's 'Hymn to Pan': a debt to Shaftesbury? *See* **5679.**
7411. SCHALL, KEITH LINWOOD. John Keats: the aesthetics of apprehension. Unpub. doct. diss., Univ. of Nevada, Reno, 1975. [Abstr. in DA (37) 5801A.]
7412. SPERRY, STUART M. Some versions of Keats. MLQ (38) 178–85 (review-article).

Fig. 30. *Annual Bibliography of English Language and Literature* 1977: 415.

With publication delayed several years, *ABELL* is less current than the printed version of the *MLA Bibliography*, much less current than the *Humanities Index*. In a thorough search of English language materials, however, you should consult both *ABELL* and the *MLA Bibliography*, because some titles cited in one are not in the other.

The Year's Work in English Studies is more selective than either *ABELL* or the *MLA Bibliography*. For each literary period in English and American literature, for a few general subjects, and for Chaucer, Shakespeare, and Milton, it offers bibliographic essays on important criticism published during the preceding year. The subject index at the end of each volume directs you to the portions of the essays that deal with particular authors or works. For example, the index to volume 65, covering 1983, tells you that some discussion of the literary criticism on Toni Morrison's *Tar Baby* appears on page 656 (fig. 31). Although many users find the essay format a bit cumbersome, the author of each essay does glean the noteworthy studies from all the critical chaff of that year and does provide some indication of their contents (fig. 32). However, the publication delay of several years dilutes the usefulness of this bibliography.

Morris, William, **440**, **470–1**, 472, **480–1**;
and Dallas, 484–5; and St Dorothea,
444; and Ruskin, 483; and landscape,
417; and the socialist press, 487; and
Young England, 481; lectures, 481;
letters, 480; poetry, 18, 440; politics,
440; reviews, 481; socialist prose, 481;
Victorian criticism of, 472; 'Art and
Labour', 480; 'Art and Socialism',
481; 'Art Under Plutocracy', 481; *The
Earthly Paradise*, 440, 472; German
Romances, 471; 'The Lesser Arts',
481; 'London in a State of Siege', 481;
News from Nowhere, 471, 480;
'Wanderers' Prologue', 440
Morrison, Toni, 605, **656**, 763; *Song of
Solomon*, 656; *The Tar Baby*, 656
Morte Arthur, stanzaic, 118

Fig. 31. *The Year's Work in English Studies* 65: 924.

656   TWENTIETH-CENTURY AMERICAN LITERATURE

To conclude this section a number of articles should be noted on lesser-known contemporary novelists. John G. Parks (*TCL*) discusses Shirley Jackson's own particular variations on the Gothic mode, particularly the ways in which a disintegrating world forces her female protagonists into fantasy or madness. Charles H. Adams (*Crit*) chooses a rather older novel – W. M. Kelley's *A Different Drummer* (1962) – and finds gloom there about the possibility of a black community. Natalie Maynor and Richard F. Patteson (*Crit*) look at Russell Hoban's creation of a postholocaust dialect in *Riddley Walker* (1980) to evoke a regression to the primitive. The novels of Toni Morrison attract three critics. Peter B. Erickson surveys patterns of imagery in *The Tar Baby* (*CLAJ*), locating preoccupations with female sexuality and motherhood as the sources of narrative momentum. Elizabeth B. House (*AL*) also looks for patterns in the fictions but her preferences go to the repeated contrasts between idyllic dreams and the 'competitive acquisition of power or money'. Robert James Butler (*CentR*) relates Morrison's *Song of Solomon* to the tradition of mobility in American literature. He identifies a dialectical structure in the novel 'between the possibilities of space and the securities of place'.

Fig. 32. *The Year's Work in English Studies* 65: 656.

6.
Special Indexes and Bibliographies

a. Bibliographies by Genre

Over the years, a number of special bibliographies have been produced that can save you a great deal of research time. Each concentrates on a particular literary genre, giving you a convenient list of literary criticism on specific poems, plays, novels, or short stories. As you have seen, the *Humanities Index* and the *MLA Bibliography* are not always helpful with titles that have not received much critical attention. In contrast, the genre bibliographies provide thorough coverage of less prominent literary works in addition to offering a good list of criticism on the best-known.

For example, if you consult Kuntz and Martinez's *Poetry Explication* for discussions of Keats's "To Autumn," you find twenty-two items for that poem (fig. 33). *Poetry Explication* lists literary criticism published between 1925 and 1977, providing a timesaving compilation of fifty-two years of research in periodicals, books, and parts of books. There you discover, for example, that Michael Cooke has a four-page discussion of the Keats ode in his 1976 book, *The Romantic Will*, and you learn that Donald Pearce writes about the poem at length in a 1975 article "Thoughts on the Autumn Ode of Keats" (fig. 33). At the end of their guide, Kuntz and Martinez provide complete bibliographic information, including the author's full name, the publisher, and the date of publication, for every book cited in the checklist.

As the title implies, *English Novel Explication*, by Palmer and Dyson, compiles criticism of individual British novels. Because it supplements an earlier source, *The English Novel, 1578-1958*, by Bell and Baird, it includes only studies printed between 1958 and 1972. It, too, has had three supplements, although by different authors, bringing the coverage up to 1984. Although the format of *English Novel Explication* is similar to that of *Poetry Explication* and both conclude with complete lists of the books indexed, Palmer and Dyson supply somewhat more data for the book entries within the bibliography itself. For example, as figure 34 shows, the one book cited for Thomas Hardy's *Tess of the D'Urbervilles* includes the author's full name and the year of publication: Jean R. Brooks's *Thomas Hardy: The Poetic Structure*.

Coleman and Tyler's *Drama Criticism* is a checklist of explications, published between 1940 and 1964, that deal with English and American plays. This bibliography is particularly useful for prolific writers such as Shake-

```
  "To Autumn"
Bloom, The Visionary Company, pp. 421-425.

Brooks, Purser, and Warren, An Approach to Literature, fourth edition,
pp. 419-420.

Brower, The Fields of Light, pp. 39-41.

Irving H. Buchen, "Keats's 'To Autumn': The Season of Optimum Form,"
CEA, 31 (Nov., 1968), 11.

Michael G. Cooke, The Romantic Will (New Haven and London:  Yale Univ.
Press, 1976), pp. 170-174.

Robert Daniel and Monroe C. Beardsley, "Reading Takes a Whole Man," CE,
17 (Oct., 1955), 31-32.

Eugene Green and Rosemary M. Green, "Keats's Use of Names in Endymion and
in the Odes," SIR, 16 (Winter, 1977), 32-34.

Norman Hampson, "Keats and Ourselves," TLS, Dec. 22, 1945, p. 607.

Geoffrey H. Hartman, "Poem and Ideology:  A Study of Keats's 'To Autumn,'"
in Literary Theory and Structure:  Essays in Honor of William K. Wimsatt,
ed. Frank Brady, John Palmer, and Martin Price (New Haven:  Yale Univ.
Press, 1973), pp. 305-330.

Knight, The Starlit Dome, pp. 300-301.

F. R. Leavis, "Keats (Revaluations IX)," Scrutiny, 4 (March, 1936), 392-
393.

Leavis, Revaluation, pp. 262-264.

James Lott, "Keats's To Autumn:  The Poetic Consciousness and the Awareness
of Process," SIR, 9 (Winter, 1970), 71-81.

Anna Jean Mill, "Keats and Ourselves," TLS, Feb. 2, 1946, p. 55.

Donald Pearce, "Thoughts on the Autumn Ode of Keats," ArielE, 6 (July,
1975), 3-19.

Perkins, The Quest for Permanence, pp. 290-294.

Rosenheim, What Happens in Literature, pp. 42-59.

Satin, Reading Poetry, pp. 1102-1104.

B. C. Southam, "The Ode 'To Autumn,'" KSJ, 9, Part 2 (Autumn, 1960), 91-
98.

Leonard Unger, "Keats and the Music of Autumn," Western Review, 14 (Sum-
mer, 1950), 275-284.
   Rpt. The Man in the Name, pp. 18-29.

Unger and O'Connor, Poems for Study, pp. 454-456.
   Rpt. Locke, Gibson, and Arms, Introduction to Literature, fourth edi-
   tion, pp. 109-110.
   Rpt. fifth edition, pp. 102-103.

Walsh, The Use of Imagination, pp. 119-120.
```

Fig. 33. Joseph M. Kuntz and Nancy C. Martinez, *Poetry Explication: A Checklist of Interpretations since 1925 of British and American Poems Past and Present*, 3rd ed. 274-75.

Tess of the D'Urbervilles, 1891

Andersen, Carol Reed, Time, Space and Perspective in Thomas Hardy, Nineteenth Century Fiction (Dec. 1954), 9: 192-208

Bailey, J. O., Hardy's Visions of the Self, Studies in Philology (Jan. 1959), 56:74-101

Baker, Ernest A., The History of the English Novel. Vol. 9. 1938. p. 68-75

Brick, Allan, Paradise and Consciousness in Hardy's "Tess," Nineteenth Century Fiction (Sept. 1962), 17:115-34

Brooks, Jean R., Thomas Hardy; The Poetic Structure. 1971. p. 233-53

Carpenter, Richard C., Hardy's "Gurgoyles," Modern Fiction Studies (1960), 6:223-32

Fig. 34. Helen H. Palmer and Anne J. Dyson, *English Novel Explication: Criticism to 1972* 149.

speare, because it furnishes a single compilation of twenty-four years of older literary criticism about each of his plays. The more current *Dramatic Criticism Index*, by Breed and Sniderman, is restricted to twentieth-century playwrights, from Ibsen to the avant-garde.

A genre bibliography is probably the most helpful tool for locating treatments of specific short stories. Since such criticism is usually published as part of a book or as a journal article, it is difficult to find in a card or online catalog or in printed versions of the indexes and bibliographies discussed in the previous chapters. For this reason, Warren Walker's *Twentieth-Century Short Story Explication* is very valuable. Notice that many of the items supplied for "The Pupil," by Henry James, are only a few pages in books about James's work in general (fig. 35). Now in its third edition, with three supplements, Walker's bibliography is current through 1984.

Other genre bibliographies are noted in the appendix to this guide. As discussed in chapter 1, the *Literary Criticism Index* leads directly to the relevant parts of many of these sources. Genre bibliographies can give you an excellent starting point, but they become increasingly outdated with each passing year. For current materials, you need to rely on the quarterly, semiannual, or annual indexes and bibliographies, such as the *Essay and General Literature Index*, the *Humanities Index*, and the *MLA Bibliography*, or their electronic versions.

"The Pupil"
   Booth, Wayne C. *The Rhetoric of Fiction*, 365-366.
   Canavan, Thomas L. "The Economics of Disease in James's 'The Pupil,'" *Criticism*, 15 (1973), 253-264.
   Cummins, Elizabeth. "'The Playroom of Superstition': An Analysis of Henry James's 'The Pupil,'" *Markham R*, 2 (May, 1970), 13-16.
   Edel, Leon, Ed. . . . *Selected Fiction*, 480-481.
   Fadiman, Clifton, Ed. *The Short Stories* . . . , 268-272.
   Geismar, Maxwell. *Henry James* . . . , 114-117.
   Griffith, John. "James's 'The Pupil' As Whodunit: The Question of Moral Responsibility," *Stud Short Fiction*, 9 (1972), 257-268.
   Gross, Theodore L. *The Heroic Ideal* . . . , 78-79.
   Hagopian, John V. "Seeing Through 'The Pupil' Again," *Mod Fiction Stud*, 5 (1959), 169-171; rpt. in part Stone, Edward, Ed. *Henry James* . . . , 191-193.
   Hoffmann, Charles G. *The Short Novels* . . . , 52.
   Howe, Irving, Ed. . . . *Modern Fiction*, 217-225.
   James, Henry. *What Maisie Knew* . . . , xv-xviii; rpt. in his . . . *Critical Prefaces*, 150-154; pb. ed., 150-154; Edel, Leon, Ed. *Henry James* . . . , 476-480; rpt. in part Stone, Edward, Ed. *Henry James* . . . , 183-185.
   Jefferson, D. W. *Henry James* . . . , 146-150.
   Kenney, William. "The Death of Morgan in James's 'The Pupil,'" *Stud Short Fiction*, 8 (1971), 317-322.

Fig. 35. Warren S. Walker, *Twentieth-Century Short Story Explication: Interpretations, 1900–1975, of Short Fiction since 1800*, 3rd ed. 373.

b. Bibliographies by Literary Period

As you can see from the preceding section, a ready-made bibliography can be enormously valuable. In addition to bibligraphies by genre, several are available for literary periods. A few, which you may already have discovered through the *Bibliographic Index* or the card or online catalog, are worth special, if brief, mention at this point.

The standard bibliography for British literature is *The New Cambridge Bibliography of English Literature* (*NCBEL*), a comprehensive tool that covers both primary and secondary sources for English literature from 600 to 1950. Leary's *Articles on American Literature* indexes seventy-five years of criticism on American literature, arranged by literary period. These works may exceed your present needs, but you might keep them in mind for more extensive research at a later date.

For many literary periods and several authors, there exists a series of bibliographies that are sufficiently selective to be especially useful for term-paper research. The Goldentree Bibliographies in Language and Literature are found in most college libraries; the subjects covered are listed in the appendix.

c. Indexes to Book Reviews

You may be unable to locate much literary criticism on a work if it has been published so recently that no substantial body of scholarship has yet become available. In this circumstance none of the indexes and bibliographies discussed so far in this guide is going to prove very helpful. The only treatment of a recent work may be a book or play review in a current (perhaps even popular) periodical or newspaper. For such criticism you can consult indexes to book reviews.

The two major indexes of this sort are *Book Review Digest* and *Book Review Index*. Although the *Digest* began publication in 1905, sixty years earlier than the *Index*, its coverage is much more limited than that of its younger rival. Before any review for a work of fiction is listed in *Book Review Digest*, at least four reviews of the book must have been published in the periodicals indexed. At the same time, *Book Review Digest* is very up-to-date, published quarterly with annual cumulations. The *Digest*'s editors sometimes furnish brief excerpts from the more important reviews, and they provide word counts so that you know whether a review is simply a short paragraph or a substantial essay. Since April 1983 electronic access to *Book Review Digest* has been available through the data bases Wilsonline and Wilsondisc, discussed in chapter 4. Once again the microcomputer offers greater speed and efficiency. If, for example, you were looking for criticism of Toni Morrison's *Beloved* in 1987, the year the novel was published, you would proba-

```
BBRD87005665
Book Review
871118
Morrison, Toni:1931-
Beloved; a novel
Personal Name Main Entry
Knopf:us
1987
us
Language: English
275
0-394-53597-9:$18.95
Fiction
LC Class No: PS3563.08749:B4 1987
LC Card No: 86-46157
Subject heading: Fiction themes/Slavery
Subject heading: Fiction themes/Locality/Ohio
Subject heading: Fiction themes/Locality/Kentucky
In this novel set in Ohio after the end of the Civil War, Sethe,
who eighteen years earlier had fled from slavery on a Kentucky
plantation, is haunted by the spirit of Beloved, the two-year-old
daughter she had killed when threatened with recapture.  The
baby's ghost is driven from Sethe's home, but then, along comes a
strange, beautiful, real flesh-and-blood young woman, about 20
years old, who can't seem to remember where she comes from, who
talks like a young child, who has an odd, raspy voice and no
lines on her hands, who takes an intense, devouring interest in
Sethe, and who says her name is Beloved.  (N Y Times Book Rev)
    Library Journal 112:201 S 1 '87 Fisher, Ann H. 130w
      Powerful is too tame a word to describe Toni Morrison's
      searing new novel. . . . A fascinating, grim, relentless
      story, this important book by a major writer belongs in
      most libraries.
    The New York Times Book Review p:1: S 13 '87 Atwood, Margaret
      2900w
      Ms. Morrison's versatility and technical and emotional range

      appear to know no bounds. . . . :This book is: a
      hair-raiser. . . . The supernatural element is treated .
      . . with magnificent practicality. . . . Through the
      different voices and memories of the book. . . . we
      experience American slavery as it was lived by those who
      were its objects of exchange. . . . Beloved' is written
      in an antiminimalist prose that is by turns rich,
      graceful, eccentric, rough, lyrical, sinuous, colloquial
      and very much to the point. . . . In this book, the other
      world exists and magic works, and the prose is up to it.
      If you can believe page one--and Ms. Morrison's verbal
      authority compels belief--you're hooked on the rest of
      the book.
    Newsweek 110:74 S 28 '87 Clemons, Walter 1300w
      :In this: magnificent novel, . . . :a slave's: interior life
      is re-created with a moving intensity no novelist has
      even approached before. . . . The splintered, piecemeal
      revelation of the past is one of the technical wonders of
      Morrison's narrative.  We gradually understand that this
      isn't tricky storytelling but the intricate exploration
      of trauma. . . . Morrison casts a formidable spell.  The
      incantatory, intimate narrative voice disarms our
      reluctance to enter Sethe's haunted house.  We are
      reassured by feeling that the eerie story is reinforced
      by exact attention to verifiable detail. . . . The flood
      of daylight that ends the book is overpowering.  I think
      we have a masterpiece on our hands here: difficult,
      sometimes lushly overwritten, but profoundly imagined and
      carried out with burning fervor.
    Time 130:75 S 21 '87 Gray, Paul 1200w
      The flesh-and-blood presence of Beloved roils the novel's
      intense, realistic surface.  This young woman may not
      actually be Sethe's reincarnated daughter, but no other
      explanation of her identity is provided.  Her symbolic
      significance is confusing: she seems to represent both
      Sethe's guilt and redemption.  And Morrison's attempt to
      make this strange figure come to life strains
      unsuccessfully toward the rhapsodic: I will never leave
      you again/ Don't ever leave me again/ You will never
      leave me again.'  In the end, the implausibilities in
      Beloved may matter less than the fact that Sethe believes
      them.  Uneducated, her heritage and culture reduced to a
      few shreds of memory, she sees no distinction between the
      supernatural and the equally surreal facts of her own
      life.  Morrison's heroine is hard to understand, and to
      forget.
    Ms. 16:66 N '87 Gillespie, Marcia Ann 500w
    The Nation 245:418 O 17 '87 Brown, Rosellen 2850w
    The Christian Science Monitor (Eastern edition) p20 O 5 '87
      Rubin, Merle 850w
    Commonweal 114:631 N 6 '87 Baker-Fletcher, Karen 1000w
    The New York Review of Books 34:18 N 5 '87 Edwards, Thomas R.
      3300w
    The New Republic 197:38 O 19 '87 Crouch, Stanley 5000w
      :Beloved: explains black behavior in terms of social
      conditioning, as if listing atrocities solves the mystery
      of human motive and behavior.  It is designed to placate
      sentimental feminist ideology, and to make sure that the
      vision of black woman as the most scorned and rebuked of
      the victims doesn't weaken. . . . :The author: has real

      talent, an ability to organize her novel in a musical
      structure, deftly using images as motifs; but she
      perpetually interrupts her narrative with maudlin
      ideological commercials. . . . Morrison rarely gives the
      impression that her people exist for any purpose other
      then to deliver a message. . . . Crass obvious . . . wins
      out over Morrison's literary gift at every significant
      turn.
    The New Yorker 63:175 N 2 '87 Thurman, Judith 3000w
    Quill & Quire 53:30 N '87 Stuewe, Paul 170w
    National Review 43:54 D 4 '87 Mano, D. Keith 1100w
1987
```

Fig. 36. From *Book Review Digest* on Wilsonline.

bly have found that the printed version of *Book Review Digest* had not yet picked up many reviews. A quick search on Wilsonline, however, would reveal fourteen items (fig. 36). Notice that several of these reviews, especially those in the *New York Times Book Review*, *Nation*, *New Republic*, and *New York Review of Books*, are quite long.

Although *Book Review Index* provides neither excerpts from reviews nor word counts, it indexes more periodicals than *Book Review Digest* does. In addition, *Book Review Index* sets no minimum number of reviews as a criterion for inclusion. To be listed, a book need only have been reviewed in one of the periodicals covered. Thus, in searching for reviews of Morrison's *Beloved*, you would find more citations in *Book Review Index* for the fourth quarter of 1987 (fig. 37) than you would in the equivalent printed version of *Book Review Digest*. Since 1969 the *Index* has also been available online through Dialog, discussed in chapter 5.

Even reviews that date back a number of years can be consulted for contemporary fiction. You can compare reviews written for popular periodicals shortly after a novel's publication with criticism that appears later in scholarly journals, reflecting more years of study.

Of course, indexes to book reviews also compile reviews of nonfiction. These commentaries can indicate how a book of literary criticism was received at the time of its publication. If, for example, you were preparing a paper on "To Autumn," and planning to use Michael Cooke's *Romantic Will* (a book you found earlier through *Poetry Explication*), you might want to read reviews of this study to learn what other Keats scholars think of it. While *Book Review Digest* and *Book Review Index* can supply some citations,

> **Morrison, Toni** - *Beloved*
> y   BL - v83 - Jl '87 - p1627
>   CSM - v79 - O 5 '87 - p20
>   KR - v55 - Jl 15 '87 - p1023
>   LATBR - Ag 30 '87 - p1
>   LJ - v112 - S 1 '87 - p201
>   Nat - v245 - O 17 '87 - p418
>   New R - v197 - O 19 '87 - p38
>   NW - v110 - 9 '87 - p74
>   NYT - v136 - S 2 '87 - p19
>   NYTBR - v92 - S 13 '87 - p1
>   Obs - O 11 '87 - p27
>   PW - v232 - Jl 17 '87 - p53
>   Time - v130 - S 21 '87 - p75
>   TLS - O 16 '87 - p1135
>   Trib Bks - Ag 2 '87 - p3
>   Trib Bks - Ag 30 '87 - p1
>   USA T - v5 - S 4 '87 - p6D
>   VLS - S '87 - p25

Fig. 37. *Book Review Index* Sept.-Dec. 1987: 225.

two other indexes are better suited to this kind of research problem. *An Index to Book Reviews in the Humanities*, because it indexes reviews from over 675 scholarly journals, is far more likely to pick up erudite evaluations of serious studies like Cooke's. In fact, the 1977 volume of this index cites a review of *The Romantic Will* in the *Times Literary Supplement* (fig. 38). A second excellent choice would be the *Annual Bibliography of English Language and Literature*, which, you recall from the preceding chapter, notes book reviews with its entries for critical works. *ABELL* would be another logical place in which to look for reviews of Cooke's study. By the way, the *Humanities Index*, discussed in chapter 4, also has a list of book reviews in the final section of each issue.

```
COOKE, A.  SIX MEN.
  J. RESTON, 441:25SEP77-10
  C. SIGAL, 362:8DEC77-750
COOKE, K.  A.C. BRADLEY & HIS INFLU-
  ENCE IN TWENTIETH-CENTURY SHAKE-
  SPEARE CRITICISM.*
  C.M. SHAW, 570(SQ):WINTER75-84
COOKE, M.  THE ROMANTIC WILL.
  J. BAYLEY, 617(TLS):17JUN77-718
COOKSON, W. - SEE POUND, E.
COOLE, A.B.  THE EARLY COINS OF THE
  CHOU DYNASTY.
  R.C. HOUSTON, 318(JAOS):JUL-SEP75-
  526
COOLEY, P.  THE COMPANY OF STRANGERS.
  N.J. HERRINGTON, 584(SWR):SPRING76-
  213
  H. THOMAS, 385(MQR):WINTER77-94
```

Fig. 38. *An Index to Book Reviews in the Humanities* 18: 79.

7.
Other Reference Tools

a. Biographical Sources

For most of your term papers, you may not need biographical information on the authors studied in the course or on the critics who wrote about them. But occasionally a few biographical facts can shed additional light on an author's work or on a research problem. Many reference books discuss the lives of English and American writers. Some supply only a brief paragraph or two of basic data—dates and places of birth and death, major works, and the like. Others offer lengthy treatments of each author's life and literary accomplishments.

The *Dictionary of National Biography* (*DNB*), edited by Leslie and Lee, falls into the latter category. Large and definitive, authoritative and readable, the *DNB* describes the lives and work of British writers as well as of Britons famous in other occupations. The length of each biographical account is proportionate to the importance of the subject. Shakespeare is awarded forty-nine pages; Keats only fifteen.

The equivalent of the *DNB* on this side of the Atlantic is the *Dictionary of American Biography* (*DAB*). Like its British counterpart, the *DAB* discusses at some length prominent deceased Americans of all professions. Critics of the *DAB* have lamented that many distinguished American women are absent from its pages. In fact, *Notable American Women* (*NAW*), a four-volume companion to the *DAB*, has been published specifically to compensate for these omissions. For biographies of deceased American women writers, you should look in both the *DAB* and the *NAW*.

If you need information on a writer who was alive when these sources were published, you should turn to *Current Biography*. Issued monthly and cumulated annually, it details the lives and achievements of famous persons in all professions around the world. Writers are well represented.

Contemporary Authors is a multivolume biographical encyclopedia specifically devoted to living writers. International in scope, it covers authors of works in various fields, including literature. Treatments are generally briefer than those in the *DNB, DAB, NAW,* and *Current Biography*. But *Contemporary Authors* does have information about most writers on the current scene.

The single-volume biographical dictionaries of literary figures mentioned in the appendix are more restrictive in scope and coverage, affording each author a factual paragraph or two. But for basic data, they may be perfectly adequate.

43

Don't forget that you can find biographies of individual authors in the card or online catalog. Most general encyclopedias, like *Encyclopedia Americana* and *Encyclopaedia Britannica*, have biographical information, too.

b. In Quest of Quotations

In writing your term paper, you will undoubtedly use quotations from your primary source as documentation for your thesis. Most likely you will have noted the important passages in your copy of the novel, poem, play, or short story. But once or twice you will need to track down an elusive quotation to substantiate a point you wish to make.

Two kinds of reference sources can assist you in the hunt for specific quotations. The first of these, the concordance, is an alphabetical index to all substantial words in an individual work or in a body of works. Concordances exist to different versions of the *Bible* and to the works of many major authors, such as Shakespeare. It is easy to appreciate the usefulness of this type of reference tool. If you were looking for the line in *Hamlet* "there is special providence in the fall of a sparrow," you could waste considerable time and energy thumbing randomly through your copy of the play, or you could consult *The Harvard Concordance to Shakespeare*. To track down the quotation in the concordance, you simply check the choices under one of the three keywords in the line: *fall, providence,* and *sparrow*. The word *fall* is so common that certainly too many quotations would appear under that term to make the line easy to find. In fact, *The Harvard Concordance to Shakespeare* has three columns of choices under *fall*. Under *providence*, however, there are only six quotations, the sixth being the one you want (fig. 39). It is *Hamlet*, act 5, scene 2, line 220. The P following the citation in the concordance indicates a prose passage as opposed to one in verse. The age of computerization has brought an assortment of concordances to complement various works and authors. If your library has a concordance to the work of a specific author, the formal subject heading in the card or online catalog is under

PROVIDENCE		6 FR	0.0006 REL FR	5 V	1 P
by providence divine.			TMP	1.02.159	
but by immortal providence she's mine.				5.01.189	
the providence that's in a watchful state			TRO	3.03.196	
to stay the providence of some high powers			JC	5.01.106	
us, whose providence I should have kept short,			HAM	4.01. 17	
there is special providence in the fall of a				5.02.220 P	
PROVIDENT		2 FR	0.0002 REL FR	2 V	0 P

Fig. 39. Marvin Spevack, *The Harvard Concordance to Shakespeare* 1022.

the author's name and the subdivision "—Concordance," as in "Shakespeare, William, 1564-1616—Concordance." If your online catalog permits free text searching with Boolean operators, the terms *Shakespeare* and *Concordance*, joined by an *and*, should identify the title you seek.

You are not going to find a concordance for every author. If a quotation is fairly well known, it may appear in a dictionary of general quotations, such as *The Oxford Dictionary of Quotations* or Bartlett's *Familiar Quotations*. Each of them has a keyword index to appropriate authors and sources. All these dictionaries, some of which are mentioned in the appendix, are selective, but all include some important quotations from literature. And, as you will see in the next section, one special English-language dictionary, the *Oxford English Dictionary*, has recently been transformed, through computerization, into a dictionary of quotations.

c. Facts from Dictionaries and Handbooks

When you need quick information, such as the definition of a word or the history of a literary concept, you head for an English-language dictionary or a literary handbook. You probably already own an abridged English-language dictionary. Good, inexpensive versions in hard or soft covers have been available from Merriam-Webster, Random House, and Funk and Wagnalls for years. They usually suffice for everyday problems of spelling, pronunciation, and definition. When a desk-size version fails to solve your problem, an unabridged dictionary, like *Webster's Third New International Dictionary of the English Language*, should be your next recourse. While abridged dictionaries are limited to the most frequently used words, the unabridged strive to include all known words in the language with the possible exceptions of some slang or colloquial terms. Your college library has an ample supply of both abridged and unabridged dictionaries.

As you study literature from earlier centuries, an etymological dictionary will prove invaluable. For every word ever known to exist, this kind of dictionary supplies a history, the date of its first known recorded use, variant spellings and pronunciations, and distinctive usages. The multivolume *Oxford English Dictionary* (*OED*) is an excellent example. If you wanted to examine the possible meanings of the term *nunnery* in Hamlet's famous command to Ophelia, "Get thee to a nunnery!" (*Hamlet* 3.1.121), you would have to consult the *OED*. According to this dictionary, the term can mean either a residence for nuns or "a house of ill fame" (fig. 40). Since the second usage was apparently introduced by Nashe in 1593, it would have been known during Shakespeare's time. The last volume of the *OED* provides full bibliographic information on Nashe's work as well as on other sources cited throughout the dictionary.

Since 1987 all twelve volumes of the *OED* have been available on two CD–ROM disks that can be read through the use of a microcomputer linked to a CD–ROM drive. Unlike the printed version that limits your access solely

Nunnery (nʋ'něri). Forms: a. 3–7 non-nerie, 3–5 -erye, 4, 6 nonery, 6 noonery. β. 4, 7 nunnerie, 5 nvnnerye, 6- nunnery (7 nunery). [Prob. ad. AF. *nonnerie, f. nonne NUN *sb.*¹: see -ERY. Cf. F. nonnerie (Littré).]

1. A place or residence for a body or community of nuns; a building in which nuns live under religious rule and discipline; a convent.

a. *c* **1275** LAY. 15642 Nou was Merlyn his moder..in one nonnerie munechene ihoded. *c* **1290** *S. Eng. Leg.* I. 91/148 hir nortelrye, That sche had lerned in a nonnerye. *c* **1425** *Hampole's Psalter* Metr. Pref. 28 Þar it ly3t in cheyn bondes in þe same nonery. **1470–85** MALORY *Arthur* XXI. ix. 854 Atte last he cam to a nonnerye. **1523** LD. BERNERS *Froiss.* I. cxxv. 151 The kyng of Englande was at Poissoy, and lay in the nonery there. *c* **1611** *Women Saints* 55 Her sister St. Etheldred..founder of that Nonnerie.

β. *c* **1305** *Land Cokayne* 147 An oþer abbei is þerbi For soth a gret fair nunnerie. **1483** *Cath. Angl.* 257/1 A Nvnnerye, *cenobium.* **1571** A. JENKINSON *Voy. & Trav.* (Hakl. Soc.) I. 137 Not farre from the said Castle was a Nunnery of sumptuous building. **1602** SHAKS. *Ham.* III. i. 122 Get thee to a Nunnerie. *Ibid.* 132 Goe thy wayes to a Nunnery. **1648** GAGE *West Ind.* 58 This man alone built a Nunery of Franciscan Nuns. *a* **1699** LADY HALKETT *Autobiog.* (Camden) 15 That there was a nunery in Holland for those of the Protestant relligion. **1707** LADY M. W. MONTAGU *Lett.* II. xlvii. 43 Her relations..would certainly confine her to a nunnery for the rest of her days. **1756–7** tr. *Keysler's Trav.* (1760) II. 229 There are boards placed before most of the windows, like those in a great many nunneries. **1841** ELPHINSTONE *Hist. Ind.* I. 201 Nunneries for women seem also, at one time, to have been general. **1886** *Pall Mall G.* 17 July 5/2 To the south-east we may see the ruins of Sopwell nunnery.

fig. **1634** HABINGTON *Castara* I. (Arb.) 18 Yee blushing Virgins [*sc.* roses] happie are In the chaste Nunn'ry of her brests. **1652** CRASHAW *Elegy Mr. Stanninow*, Whose nest Was in the modest Nunnery of his brest.

attrib. **1859** TENNYSON *Guinev.* 225 O little maid, shut in by nunnery walls. **1884** J. HALL *Christian Home* 113 When no safety could be hoped for California girls but in nunnery schools.

b. *transf.* A house of ill fame.

1593 NASHE *Christ's T.* 79 b, [To] some one Gentleman generally acquainted, they giue..free priuiledge thenceforward in theyr Nunnery, to procure them frequentance. **1617** FLETCHER *Mad Lover* IV. ii, Theres an old Nunnerie at hand. What's that? A bawdy-house. **17**.. (*title-p.*), The Complete London Spy, or Disclosures of the Transactions in and around London and Westminster Coffee houses, Nunneries, Night Houses, Taverns, Bagnios, etc.

†2. The institution of conventual life for women; nunship. *Obs.*

1650 FULLER *Pisgah* II. iii. § 11. 95 *marg.*, Nicolas Lyra *in locum*, with most Roman commentators since his time, in hope to found Nunnery thereupon. **1679** PRANCE *Add. Narrative* 11 English Gentlewomen,..who have a mind to take the Vail of Nunnery upon them.

Fig. 40. *Oxford English Dictionary* 7: 264.

to looking up a specific word, the *OED* on CD–ROM offers more search paths than just the lemma (the headword for each entry). You can seek out an etymology, a definition, a part of speech, a subject category, a place name, or a quotation. To find a quotation, you can ask the computer to search for the quotation itself or for its date, author, or source. In other words, the *OED* on CD–ROM is not just the standard etymological dictionary of the English language but also a powerful dictionary of quotations — another excellent example of the way in which automation can make an important reference work even more useful.

For general information on an author or a literary period, for the identification of characters, or for the definition of literary terms, a handbook is your best tool. *The Oxford Companion to English Literature* and *The Oxford Companion to American Literature* are excellent, easy-to-use, single-volume handbooks. Each has basic biographical information about authors, brief plot summaries of major works, short definitions of literary terms and concepts, and general outlines of literary movements. These two handbooks focus on a nationality; others, like the *Princeton Encyclopedia of Poetry and Poetics*, are organized around a genre. For a term paper on Keats, for example, you might want to look up *ode* in the *Princeton Encyclopedia*, which defines the term and gives a history of the form from the Greek poets through modern times (fig. 41). At the end of the entry, there is even a brief bibliography of major works on the ode. It is a good idea to consult a handbook whenever you do not clearly understand some term. Other literary handbooks and English language dictionaries are noted in the appendix.

d. Guidelines on Form

As you prepare the final draft of your term paper, you will undoubtedly want to make sure that your work, especially its documentation and bibliography, is presented in an acceptable form. The *MLA Handbook for Writers of Research Papers* describes the conventions for written literary research that are approved by scholars and college professors. In addition, it briefly discusses the process of selecting and researching a topic as well as the mechanics of writing critical prose. There are over a hundred examples of reference notes and bibliographic entries, intended to illustrate the citation of every conceivable kind of source that you might use. Sample pages of a research paper are given, too, to help you set up your paper according to the recommended format. A detailed index makes this handbook particularly easy to use. The *MLA Handbook* is available at your library, but if you plan to write many literary research papers, you will want to obtain your own copy.

ODE (Gr. *aeidein* "to sing," "to chant"). In modern usage the name for the most formal, ceremonious, and complexly organized form of lyric poetry, usually of considerable length. It is frequently the vehicle for public utterance on state occasions, as, for example, a ruler's birthday, accession, funeral, the unveiling or dedication of some imposing memorial or public work. The o. as it has evolved in contemporary literatures generally shows a dual inheritance from classic sources, combining the reflective or philosophic character of the Horatian o. with the occasional character of the Pindaric o. (e.g., Tennyson's *Ode on the Death of the Duke of Wellington*). Frequently elaborate and complex stanzas are used, based ultimately upon either the triadic structure of the Pindaric o. or upon imitations of or developments from it, combining great variety in length of line with ingenious rhyme schemes. The serious tone of the o. not only calls for the use of a heightened diction and enrichment by poetic device, but thus lays it open, more readily than any other lyric form, to burlesque. A third form of the modern o., the Anacreontic, is descended from the 16th-c. discovery of a group of some sixty poems, all credited to Anacreon, although the Gr. originals now appear to span a full thousand years. In general the lines are short and, in comparison with the Pindaric o., the forms simple, with the subjects being love or drinking, as in the 18th-c. song "To Anacreon in Heaven," whose tune has been appropriated for "The Star-Spangled Banner."

In Gr. literature, the odes of Pindar (522–442 B.C.) were designed for choric song and dance. The words, the sole surviving element of the total Pindaric experience, reflect the demands of the other two arts. A strophe, a complex metrical structure whose length and pattern of irregular lines varies from ode to ode, reflects a dance pattern, which is then repeated exactly in an antistrophe, the pattern being closed by an epode, or third section, of differing length and structure. Length of the o. itself (surviving examples range from fragments to nearly 300 lines) is achieved through exact metrical repetition of the original triadic pattern. These odes, written for performance in a Dionysiac theatre or perhaps in the Agora to celebrate athletic victories, frequently appear incoherent through the brilliance of imagery, abrupt shifts in subject matter, and apparent disorder of form within the individual sections. Modern criticism has answered such objections, which date from the time of Pindar himself and range through Gr. and L. to modern times, by discerning dominating images, emotional relationships between subjects, and complex metrical organization. The tone of the odes is emotional, exalted, intense, and the subject matter whatever divine myths can be adduced to the occasion being celebrated. In L. literature, the characteristic o. is associated with Horace (65–8 B.C.), who derived his forms not from Pindar but from less elaborate Gr. lyrics, through Alcaeus and Sappho. The Horatian o. is stanzaic and regular, based upon a limited number of metrical variations (Alcaics, Sapphics, etc.). It is personal rather than public, general rather than occasional, tranquil rather than intense, contemplative rather than brilliant, and intended for the reader in his library rather than for the spectator in the theatre.

Fig. 41. Alex Preminger, ed., *Princeton Encyclopedia of Poetry and Poetics* 585.

8.
Using Other Libraries

In the course of your research, you may discover that your library does not have all the books or periodicals that you want to read. As your research skills become more sophisticated, your need for materials not in your college library begin to mushroom.

Although some private colleges and universities do not open their libraries to nonaffiliated students, most academic libraries permit free use of their collections, provided that visitors do not remove any materials from the building. Many libraries in the same geographical area have even developed reciprocal borrowing privileges. Most state colleges and universities permit residents of the state to borrow books from their libraries for a small fee. Do not overlook the local public library. In some communities, particularly in large cities, the resources at the public library are more extensive than those in the college library.

In addition, your library may be able to borrow books and periodical articles for you from other libraries. While interlibrary loans are sometimes not available to undergraduates at large universities, where collections are felt to be more than adequate for undergraduate requirements, many small colleges provide this service. The interlibrary-loan process can take time, so begin your research early if you need materials from other libraries.

Your reference librarian can best inform you of interlibrary-loan policies and of any reciprocal borrowing arrangements or other privileges available at nearby libraries. He or she may be able to help you determine, before you visit another library, whether it has the materials you need for your research.

9.
Guides to Research in Literature

Throughout this guide I have concentrated on literary research, emphasizing only about thirty reference sources. Of course, many other indexes, bibliographies, dictionaries, handbooks, and related tools may become helpful as you develop your knowledge and skills in the study of English or American literature. These works are cited in literary guides that provide broader coverage than is appropriate here.

Among such books is Altick and Wright's *Selective Bibliography for the Study of English and American Literature*, which provides a much longer, yet still selective, list of reference sources and background studies. Although no annotations accompany the entries, it is a handy, reasonably up-to-date compilation.

James L. Harner's *Literary Research Guide* is the most extensive guide to research tools in British, American, and other English-language literatures. Annotations are provided for most entries, accurately describing the reference sources and evaluating their overall quality and usefulness. If you have extensive research projects or plan to attend graduate school, you should, or rather must, become familiar with this excellent book.

No discussion of research guides would be complete without some mention of Eugene Sheehy's *Guide to Reference Books*. Listing all major reference books in all disciplines, "Sheehy" is the reference librarian's right hand. It is without a doubt the one comprehensive bibliography of reference sources currently available. Some entries are annotated. Its organization, first by discipline and then by type of reference, makes it especially easy to use.

These three guides to literature, along with several others, are listed in the appendix.

Appendix
Selective Bibliography of Reference Sources for English and American Literature

In the following bibliography of reference tools, the sections are numbered to coordinate with the chapters or subdivisions that treat the types of sources listed. The asterisks designate entries that are discussed in the text.

1. Bibliographies of Bibliographies

* *Bibliographic Index: A Cumulative Bibliography of Bibliographies*. New York: Wilson, 1937– .
  This index lists substantial bibliographies (50 citations or more) published as books or as parts of books or periodicals. It covers over 2,000 periodicals, many in foreign languages. Individual authors are listed as subjects. There are no annotations. Originally published quarterly, this index now appears three times a year. Starting with the 1984 volume, it is also available through the online retrieval service Wilsonline.

Howard-Hill, Trevor H. *Bibliography of British Literary Bibliographies*. 2nd ed. Oxford: Clarendon, 1986.
  This bibliography, the first volume of the *Index to British Literary Bibliography*, lists bibliographies for English literature, from 1475 to the present, that were published after 1890 as books, substantial parts of books, or periodical articles in the English language. It is arranged by author, chronological period, region, form, genre, and subject.

Nilon, Charles. *Bibliography of Bibliographies in American Literature*. New York: Bowker, 1970.
  Like the Howard-Hill work, this bibliography includes both bibliographies published separately and those in books and periodicals. There are four main sections: bibliography, author (arranged by literary period), genre, and ancillary subjects, including children's literature, folklore, diaries, and translations.

* Weiner, Alan R., and Spencer Means. *Literary Criticism Index*. Metuchen: Scarecrow, 1984.
  This excellent tool indexes over 85 sizable bibliographies of literary criticism. It lists anonymous work first, alphabetized by title, and thereafter the arrangement is alphabetical by literary author. With the publication of more and more

bibliographies and checklists of literary criticism, such as those listed later in
this appendix, the value of reference books of this type becomes increasingly
evident.

2. The Card or Online Catalog

* *Library of Congress Subject Headings.* 10th ed. 2 vols. Washington: Library of Congress, 1986.
These volumes list the terms and phrases used as subjects in the card catalog
and as formal subject headings in online catalogs.

The National Union Catalog. Washington: Library of Congress, 1958–80. *The National Union Catalog, Pre-1956 Imprints.* London: Mansell, 1968– .
Essentially this compilation is the card catalog for the Library of Congress, the
largest library in the United States.

3. Index to Parts of Books

* *Essay and General Literature Index.* New York: Wilson, 1931– .
This semiannual index locates essays in collections, including chapters of books
in which each chapter focuses on a different specific subject. No other source
separates critical essays on individual works from the general literary criticism
on an author's total work as well as this book does. Annual volumes are cumulated every five years. The first volume includes essays published since 1900.
Coverage since 1985 is also available online through Wilsonline.

4. Periodical Indexes

* *Abstracts of English Studies.* Boulder: NCTE, 1958–80. Calgary: U of Calgary P,
1981– .
Brief summaries accompany the citations for selected important articles from
over 3,000 American and foreign periodicals focusing on English, American,
or Commonwealth literature. More recent volumes also cover other literatures
written in English. Before 1970, each issue was arranged by periodical, with
articles on different subjects grouped together. In 1970, the organization changed:
articles are now arranged by subject, literary period, and genre; and major authors
are separated within each section. There is an annual index to critics and to
subjects (including literary authors).

* *Humanities Index.* New York: Wilson, 1975– .
Entitled *International Index to Periodicals* from 1920 to 1965 and *Social Sciences and
Humanities Index* from 1965 to 1974, this index furnishes easy access to articles
in nearly 300 periodicals for the humanities. Because it features both author
and subject indexing, this tool, published quarterly and cumulated annually,
is particularly good for interdisciplinary subjects. A compilation of book reviews
concludes each issue. Citations from February 1984 to the present can be retrieved
by computer through Wilsonline and Wilsondisc, an online system and a
CD-ROM product respectively.

5. Annual Bibliographies

* *Annual Bibliography of English Language and Literature*. Cambridge: Modern Humanities Research Assn., 1921– .
  This bibliography of English and American literature indexes books, pamphlets, dissertations, and periodical articles. References to book reviews are placed alongside citations for books. The language section is arranged by subject; the literature section by literary period. The index for literary authors, subjects, and critical authors makes this bibliography particularly easy to use. The major flaw is the two- to three-year publication lag.

* *MLA International Bibliography of Books and Articles on the Modern Languages and Literatures*. New York: MLA, [1921–55], 1956– .
  From 1921 through 1955, this source listed only studies written by Americans. In 1956, it began international coverage by including writers from other countries. Since 1969, the scope has been further expanded to books, dissertations, essays in festschriften, and articles in over 2,000 international periodicals. The arrangement is first by author's nationality or language, then by literary period, and then alphabetically by author. Publication is delayed by a year. Subject indexing was introduced with the 1981 volume. Computerized access to citations from the 1964 through the current volumes is provided on the Dialog online retrieval system. Wilson also offers computerized access through Wilsonline (online retrieval) and Wilsondisc (CD–ROM).

* *The Year's Work in English Studies*. London: Murray, for the English Assn., 1921– .
  A selective critical survey of studies in English and American literature, this annual guide reviews work published in books and periodicals. Each chapter deals in essay form with a literary period or a general subject, such as the English language. Although this format can be somewhat more tedious than the standard bibliographic presentation, the essays do attempt to compare studies on the same subject. The excellent index to authors and subjects provides direct access to the pages devoted to specific authors or works. Each volume is published several years late.

6a. Bibliographies by Genre

Adelman, Irving, and Rita Dworkin. *The Contemporary Novel: A Checklist of Critical Literature on the British and American Novel since 1945*. Metuchen: Scarecrow, 1972.
This checklist cites 25 years of criticism on English and American novels, covering the period from 1945 to 1970. For each author and title, critical works are listed chronologically.

Bell, Inglis F., and Donald Baird. *The English Novel, 1578–1956: A Checklist of Twentieth-Century Criticism*. Rev. ed. Hamden: Shoe String, 1974.
This selective bibliography of twentieth-century criticism of British novels includes books and periodical articles. It is largely updated by Palmer and Dyson's *English Novel Explication*, cited below.

* Breed, Paul F., and Florence M. Sniderman, eds. *Dramatic Criticism Index: A Bibliography of Commentaries on Playwrights from Ibsen to the Avant-Garde.* Detroit: Gale, 1972.
  Nearly 12,000 entries cite criticism of plays by approximately 300 American and foreign dramatists. Organized by playwright, the checklist contains indexes of titles and of critics.

Carpenter, Charles A. *Modern Drama Scholarship and Criticism, 1966–1980: An International Bibliography.* Toronto: U of Toronto P, 1986.
  This excellent bibliography covers worldwide modern drama (since Ibsen), excluding publications in non-Roman alphabets. For each playwright it lists primary works, reference works, collections of essays, and other critical studies published during this fifteen-year period.

Cline, Gloria S., and Jeffrey A. Baker, comps. *Index to Criticism of British and American Poetry.* Metuchen: Scarecrow, 1973.
  Approximately a decade of criticism, published between 1960 and 1970, forms the core of this index. The compilers selected citations with undergraduate students in mind.

* Coleman, Arthur, and Gary R. Tyler. *Drama Criticism: A Checklist of Interpretation since 1940 of English and American Plays.* Denver: Swallow, 1966.
  This source is reasonably comprehensive up to 1964, indexing explications of texts (as opposed to performances). Although it must be updated for later materials, it should be helpful for earlier criticism of specific plays.

Dyson, Anthony E. *The English Novel: Select Bibliographical Guides.* London: Oxford UP, 1974.
  This work features bibliographic essays on 20 novelists from Bunyan to Joyce, noting best editions and critical studies.

———. *English Poetry: Select Bibliographical Guides.* London: Oxford UP, 1971.
  Dyson here offers bibliographical essays on 20 poets from Chaucer to Eliot, noting best editions and studies.

Gerstenberger, Donna L., and George Hendrick. *The American Novel 1789–1959: A Checklist of Twentieth-Century Criticism.* Denver: Swallow, 1961. Supp. by *The American Novel: A Checklist of Twentieth-Century Criticism on Novels Written since 1789: Criticism Written 1960–68.* Chicago: Swallow, 1970.
  Although limited to literary criticism published before 1968, these checklists remain invaluable tools for students of the American novel.

* Kuntz, Joseph M., and Nancy C. Martinez. *Poetry Explication: A Checklist of Interpretation since 1925 of British and American Poems Past and Present.* 3rd ed. Boston: Hall, 1980.
  A convenient index to poetry criticism published in books and journals between 1925 and 1977, this guide arranges entries by poet and then by title of poem.

* Palmer, Helen H., and Anne J. Dyson. *English Novel Explication: Criticism to 1972.*
    Hamden: Shoe String, 1973. Supp. by Peter L. Abernathy, Christian J. W.
    Kloesel, and Jeffrey R. Smitten, 1976; supp. by Christian J. W. Kloesel
    and Jeffrey R. Smitten, 1981; supp. by Christian J. W. Kloesel, 1987.
    Following the format of Bell and Baird's *English Novel,* cited above, the
    Palmer and Dyson bibliography covers the period from 1958 to 1972. The
    supplements continue the citations through 1985.

Schlueter, Paul, and June Schlueter. *The English Novel: Twentieth Century Criticism.*
    2 vols. Athens: Swallow, 1982.
    Volume 1 lists criticism on novelists from Defoe to Hardy; volume 2 continues
    with twentieth-century novelists. There is unexpectedly little overlap between
    this source and Palmer and Dyson's bibliography and supplements.

* Walker, Warren S. *Twentieth-Century Short Story Explication: Interpretations, 1900–1975,
    of Short Fiction since 1800.* 3rd ed. Hamden: Shoe String, 1977. Suppls. 1980,
    1984, 1987.
    This bibliography and its supplements provide short-story criticism published
    in books and periodicals.

Weixlmann, Joe, ed. *American Short-Fiction Criticism and Scholarship, 1959–1977: A
    Checklist.* Chicago: Swallow, 1982.
    This bibliography lists criticism on American short stories and novellas that has
    appeared in books and journals.

6b. Bibliographies by Literary Period

Goldentree Bibliographies in Language and Literature. New York: Appleton;
    Arlington Heights: AHM, 1966–79.
    The titles of the selective bibliographies in this series are *Afro-American Writers,
    The Age of Dryden, American Drama from Its Beginnings to the Present, American Litera-
    ture: Poe to Garland, American Literature through Bryant, American Novel: Sinclair Lewis
    to the Present, American Novel through Henry James* (2 eds.), *British Novel: Conrad to
    the Present, British Novel: Scott through Hardy, The British Novel through Jane Austen,
    Chaucer* (2 eds.), *Linguistics and English Linguistics* (2 eds.), *The Eighteenth Century,
    Literary Criticism: Plato through Johnson, Milton* (2 eds.), *Modern British Drama, Mod-
    ern Poetry, Old and Middle English Literature, Romantic Poets and Prose Writers, Seven-
    teenth Century: Bacon through Marvell, Shakespeare: Comedies and Sonnets, Shakespeare:
    Tragedies and Histories, Sixteenth Century: Skelton through Hooker, Tudor and Stuart Drama,*
    and *Victorian Poets and Prose Writers.*

* Leary, Lewis F. *Articles on American Literature, 1900–1950.* Durham: Duke UP, 1954.
    1950–67 supp., 1970; 1968–75 supp., 1979.
    This compilation of writings comes from the quarterly checklists in the journal
    American Literature, from the *MLA Bibliography,* and from other standard bibliog-
    raphies and indexes. Although generally organized by literary period, it is par-
    ticularly useful for thematic topics.

* *The New Cambridge Bibliography of English Literature.* 5 vols. Cambridge: Cambridge
    UP, 1969–77.
    This bibliography is the most extensive compilation of primary and secondary
    sources for English literature from 600 to 1950. Entries for each author include
    locations of manuscripts, editions of works, translations, letters, and literary criti-
    cism. The breakdown of *NCBEL* is as follows: vol. 1, 600–1660; vol. 2, 1660–1800;
    vol. 3, 1800–1900; vol. 4, 1900–50; and vol. 5, index to vols. 1–4.

Pownall, David E. *Articles on Twentieth Century Literature: An Annotated Bibliography.*
    7 vols. New York: Kraus, 1955–70, 1973–80.
    Pownall has compiled "an expanded cumulation" of the annual bibliography in
    the journal *Twentieth Century Literature.*

Woodress, James L. *American Literary Scholarship.* Durham: Duke UP, 1963– .
    Similar in format to *The Year's Work in English Studies,* these bibliographic essays
    provide an annual survey of research in American literature. Chapters deal with
    individual writers, literary periods, or special topics such as folklore, and the
    titles treated are selected from the *MLA Bibliography* by the authors of the essays.
    The annual supplements appear about two years late.

6c. Indexes to Book Reviews

* *Book Review Digest.* New York: Wilson, 1905– .
    To be included in this index, a work of nonfiction must have been reviewed at
    least twice; a work of fiction four times. The entries, arranged by author, often
    give brief excerpts from the reviews, both favorable and unfavorable. A word
    count indicates the length of each review. Citations from April 1983 to the present
    are accessible on Wilsonline.

* *Book Review Index.* Detroit: Gale, 1965–69, 1972– .
    More comprehensive than the *Book Review Digest,* this source lists all book reviews,
    of both fiction and nonfiction, that appear in 200 selected periodicals. But it
    dates back only to 1965 and never provides word counts or excerpts. The Dialog
    data base offers online access to this index from 1969 on.

* *An Index to Book Reviews in the Humanities.* Williamston: Thomson, 1960– .
    This annual index lists book reviews of secondary sources in the humanities from
    over 675 scholarly periodicals. It is particularly useful for tracking down schol-
    ars' responses to new literary criticism, but it provides no excerpts from the
    reviews.

7a. Biographical Sources

Biography Index: A Cumulative Index to Biographical Material in Books and Magazines.
    New York: Wilson, 1946– .
    Published quarterly, this index provides access to biographical information ap-
    pearing in over 1,700 English-language periodicals and books, including collec-

tions of biographies. It even directs the reader to citations in many standard biographical tools. Since 1984 the *Biography Index* has been accessible by computer through Wilsonline.

* *Contemporary Authors: A Biobibliographical Guide to Current Authors and Their Work.* Detroit: Gale, 1962– .
This multivolume tool furnishes biographical information on contemporary authors in many fields of the humanities, social sciences, and natural sciences. International in scope, it tries to supply personal data, career information, and a list of works for each author. To be included, an author must have had at least one book published by a reputable press.

* *Current Biography.* New York: Wilson, 1940– .
Each volume of this work has rather lengthy entries for approximately 350 prominent persons in many occupations and of many nationalities. It is published 11 times a year with bound annual cumulations.

* *Dictionary of American Biography.* 21 vols. New York: Scribner's, 1928–37. Seven supps., 1944–81.
This set contains lengthy biographical accounts of prominent deceased Americans. The articles are written and signed by authoritative contributors. There are six general indexes: names of the subjects, contributors of the biographies, birthplaces, schools, occupations, and general topics.

* *Dictionary of National Biography.* Ed. Leslie Stephens and Sidney Lee. 8 vols. London: Oxford UP, 1967–68.
The *DNB* is the British equivalent of the *DAB*. The lengthy scholarly articles on prominent Britons, including colonial Americans, are signed by their authors.

Directory of American Scholars. 8th ed. 4 vols. New York: Bowker, 1982.
This set presents brief biographical sketches of over 35,000 scholars in the fields of history, speech, literature, philosophy, drama, language, religion, and law. An index to the entire directory is in the fourth volume.

Mainiero, Lina, ed. *American Women Writers: A Critical Reference Guide from Colonial Times to the Present.* 4 vols. New York: Ungar, 1979–81.
This source provides biographical information and critical discussion on American women writers of fiction and nonfiction, "those who are known and read, and those who have been generally neglected or undervalued because they are women." A two-volume abridged edition was published in 1982.

* *Notable American Women, 1607–1950.* 3 vols. Cambridge: Harvard UP, 1971. Supp. by *Notable American Women: The Modern Period,* 1980.
Most of the 1,350 biographical accounts in the three main volumes do not duplicate material in the *DAB*.

Vinson, James, ed. *Contemporary Dramatists*. 3rd ed. New York: St. Martin's, 1982.
This tool offers brief biographical and bibliographical notes on about 300 playwrights. A list of published works appears under each entry.

————, ed. *Contemporary Novelists*. 3rd ed. New York: St. Martin's, 1982.
This volume features sketches of novelists and short-story writers since about 1940. The format is similar to that of Vinson's *Contemporary Dramatists*.

————, ed. *Contemporary Poets*. 3rd ed. New York: St. Martin's, 1980.
This source provides brief biographical and bibliographical information on some 1,000 poets writing in English. The format resembles that of Vinson's *Contemporary Dramatists*.

7b. Concordances and Quotations Indexes

* Bartlett, John. *Familiar Quotations*. 15th ed. Boston: Little, 1980.
This standard collection of quotations has a keyword index that directs the reader to their authors. Selections listed under the same author are arranged chronologically.

Magill, Frank N. *Magill's Quotations in Context*. New York: Harper, 1966. 2nd ser. New York: Harper, 1969.
Although more selective than Bartlett's and Stevenson's collections, *Magill's* supplies lengthy interpretations of each quotation's meaning. There are keyword and author indexes.

* *The Oxford Dictionary of Quotations*. 3rd ed. New York: Oxford UP, 1979.
Quotations in this work are listed alphabetically under their authors. The keyword index, produced by computer, fills over a third of the volume.

* Spevack, Marvin. *The Harvard Concordance to Shakespeare*. Cambridge: Harvard UP, 1973.
Based on the text of *The Riverside Shakespeare*, this concordance, generated by computer, picks out the keywords in all the plays and poems.

Stevenson, Burton E. *The Home Book of Quotations*. 10th ed. New York: Dodd, 1967.
This reference tool is arranged by subject and indexed by author, phrase, and keyword.

7c. Dictionaries, Encyclopedias, and Handbooks

English-Language Dictionaries

The American Heritage Dictionary of the English Language. Boston: Houghton, 1982.
This abridged dictionary attempts to guide the reader in the proper use of the language.

The Oxford Dictionary of English Etymology. Oxford: Clarendon, 1966.
  This handy yet comprehensive volume is an etymological dictionary of the English language. Each entry notes pronunciation, various meanings in chronological order, and the century during which the word was first recorded.

* *Oxford English Dictionary.* 13 vols. Oxford: Clarendon, 1933. Supps., 1972–86.
  The *OED* is the major etymological dictionary of the English language. Its purpose is to outline the history of every word recorded since 1150. Each entry includes the date of introductory use as well as variant definitions, spellings, and pronunciations over the last 800 years, with examples of printed usage. Bowker markets the *OED* on CD–ROM.

The Random House Dictionary of the English Language: College Edition. New York: Random, 1968.
  This is an abridged version of the 1966 unabridged dictionary by the same name.

Rodale, J. I. *The Synonym Finder.* Emmaus: Rodale, 1978.
  This book offers over one million synonyms in alphabetical order.

Webster's Collegiate Thesaurus. Springfield: Merriam, 1976.
  Unlike most conventional thesauri, specifically *Roget's*, this one is arranged alphabetically in dictionary format, with synonyms, antonyms, and related words and phrases following each entry.

* *Webster's Third International Dictionary of the English Language.* Springfield: Merriam, 1961.
  Unlike any previous unabridged dictionary produced by Merriam-Webster, this controversial third edition presents the language as used currently, without qualification and censorial omissions. It forgoes the earlier practice of labeling some terms incorrect, colloquial, or vulgar.

General Encyclopedias

* *Encyclopedia Americana.* 30 vols. New York: Encyclopedia Americana, 1980.
  This is a straightforward, general-purpose encyclopedia. The final volume is an index to the set.

* *The New Encyclopaedia Britannica.* 15th ed. 30 vols. Chicago: Encyclopaedia Britannica, 1980.
  The reader should first consult the 10-volume *Micropaedia*, which supplies brief information, because it also serves as an index to the longer articles in the 19-volume *Macropaedia*. The set also contains the one-volume *Propaedia*, or outline of knowledge.

Literary Handbooks

Benét, William Rose. *The Reader's Encyclopedia.* 2nd ed. New York: Crowell, 1965.
  This standard handbook contains brief articles on literary periods, movements, terms, concepts, allusions, plots, characters, and writers.

Bordman, Gerald, ed. *The Oxford Companion to American Theatre*. New York: Oxford
    UP, 1984.
    Although this handbook concentrates on the American stage as opposed to written
    drama, students of literature can find a considerable amount of information
    here, especially in the entries for several hundred major American plays.

Drabble, Margaret, ed. *The Oxford Companion to English Literature*. 5th ed. New York:
    Oxford UP, 1985.
    This guide is the British counterpart of Hart's *Oxford Companion to American Lit-
    erature*.

* Hart, James David, ed. *The Oxford Companion to American Literature*. 5th ed. New
    York: Oxford UP, 1983.
    This source provides short summaries of American literary works, definitions
    of terms, discussions of movements or trends, and brief biographies and bib-
    liographies of writers.

Hartnoll, Phyllis, ed. *The Oxford Companion to Theatre*. 4th ed. New York: Oxford
    UP, 1983.
    This handbook focuses primarily on performances, rather than on written texts,
    but it can prove useful, nonetheless, for students of literature.

Holman, Clarence Hugh, and William Harmon. *A Handbook to Literature*. 5th ed.
    New York: Macmillan, 1986.
    Alphabetically arranged with generous cross-references, this general literary
    handbook is one of the best. It defines and discusses terms and movements in
    literature and contains a particularly useful outline of British and American liter-
    ary history in the appendix.

* Preminger, Alex, ed. *Princeton Handbook of Poetic Terms*. Princeton: Princeton UP,
    1986.
    This excellent handbook of poetry discusses genres, forms, and modes. It does
    not cover individual poets or poems.

7d. Guidelines on Form

* *MLA Handbook for Writers of Research Papers*. 3rd ed. New York: MLA, 1988.
    This manual "describes a set of conventions governing the written presentation
    of research."

8. Guides to Research in Literature

* Altick, Richard D., and Andrew Wright. *Selective Bibliography for the Study of En-
    glish and American Literature*. 6th ed. New York: Macmillan, 1979.
    This standard guide "includes only bibliographies and reference works actually
    used and usable to modern scholars." The arrangement is by subject, country,
    literary period, and type of reference book. Among the special features are a

glossary of basic bibliographic and literary terms, a list of major works that should be read by every student of literature, and a chapter on how to use scholarly tools and how to examine unfamiliar reference sources.

Bell, Inglis F., and Jennifer Gallup. *A Reference Guide to English, American, and Canadian Literature*. Vancouver: U of British Columbia P, 1971.
This guide, one of the few written for undergraduate students, covers reference works by type, subject, and literary period. There are critical bibliographies for individual authors. Some entries have brief summaries.

Gohdes, Clarence L., and Sanford E. Marovitz. *Bibliographical Guide to the Study of the Literature of the U.S.A.* 5th ed. Durham: Duke UP, 1984.
Gohdes's guide is probably the best for comparative studies of American literature. The arrangement is topical, dealing with American studies in several disciplines: literature, history, art, religion, and philosophy. The entries have annotations.

* Harner, James L. *Literary Research Guide: A Guide to Reference Sources for the Study of Literatures in English and Related Topics*. New York: MLA, 1989.
This guide provides an extensive list of important reference books and periodicals on British, American, and other literatures in English. The annotations are evaluative, offering keen observations on the quality and usefulness of specific research tools.

Kennedy, Arthur Garfield, and Donald B. Sands. *A Concise Bibliography for Students of English*. 5th ed. Stanford: Stanford UP, 1972.
This subject bibliography emphasizes recent publications of use to graduate and advanced undergraduate students. It is fairly comprehensive but not annotated.

* Sheehy, Eugene. *Guide to Reference Books*. 10th ed. Chicago: ALA, 1986.
This guide provides the broadest coverage of major scholarly research tools in all disciplines. Brief annotations accompany most entries. The literature section is subdivided by type of reference source, by language or nationality, and by author. The index leads to author and subject entries as well as to nearly all title entries.